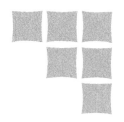

LEADING
MUSEUMS TODAY

AMERICAN ASSOCIATION FOR STATE AND LOCAL HISTORY

BOOK SERIES

ABOUT THE SERIES

The American Association for State and Local History Book Series addresses issues critical to the field of state and local history through interpretive, intellectual, scholarly, and educational texts. To submit a proposal or manuscript to the series, please request proposal guidelines from AASLH headquarters: AASLH Editorial Board, 2021 21st Ave. South, Suite 320, Nashville, TN 37212. Telephone: (615) 320-3203. Website: www.aaslh.org.

ABOUT THE ORGANIZATION

The American Association for State and Local History (AASLH) is a national history membership association headquartered in Nashville, Tennessee, that provides leadership and support for its members who preserve and interpret state and local history in order to make the past more meaningful to all people. AASLH members are leaders in preserving, researching, and interpreting traces of the American past to connect the people, thoughts, and events of yesterday with the creative memories and abiding concerns of people, communities, and our nation today. In addition to sponsorship of this book series, AASLH publishes *History News* magazine, a newsletter, technical leaflets and reports, and other materials; confers prizes and awards in recognition of outstanding achievement in the field; supports a broad education program and other activities designed to help members work more effectively; and advocates on behalf of the discipline of history. To join AASLH, go to www.aaslh.org or contact Membership Services, AASLH, 2021 21st Ave. South, Suite 320, Nashville, TN 37212.

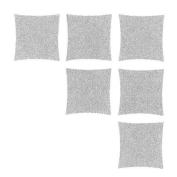

LEADING MUSEUMS TODAY

THEORY AND PRACTICE

MARTHA MORRIS

ROWMAN & LITTLEFIELD
Lanham • Boulder • New York • London

Published by Rowman & Littlefield
A wholly owned subsidary of The Rowman & Littlefield Publishing Group, Inc.
4501 Forbes Boulevard, Suite 200, Lanham, Maryland 20706
www.rowman.com

Unit A, Whitacre Mews, 26-34 Stannary Street, London SE11 4AB

British Library Cataloguing in Publication Information Available

Library of Congress Cataloging-in-Publication Data

Names: Morris, Martha (Assistant Director of Museum Studies), author.
Title: Leading museums today : theory and practice / Martha Morris.
Description: Lanham : Rowman & Littlefield, 2017. | Includes bibliographical
    references and index. | Description based on print version record and CIP
    data provided by publisher; resource not viewed.
Identifiers: LCCN 2017059166 (print) | LCCN 2018001297 (ebook) | ISBN
    9781442275348 (Electronic) | ISBN 9781442275324 (cloth : alk. paper) |
    ISBN 9781442275331 (pbk. : alk. paper)
Subjects: LCSH: Museums—Management. | Museums—Personnel management.
    | Leadership. | Leadership—Case studies. | Museums—Management—Case
    studies. | Museums—Personnel management—Case studies.
Classification: LCC AM121 (ebook) | LCC AM121 .M66 2017 (print) | DDC
    069/.068—dc23
LC record available at https://lccn.loc.gov/2017059166

Printed in the United States of America

CONTENTS

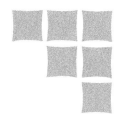

LIST OF ILLUSTRATIONS

PREFACE

B **ack at the** dawn of the information age, I attended a black tie gala event at the National Building Museum in Washington, DC. This was during the day when *Computerworld* collaborated with the Smithsonian on an annual awards program for leaders in the technology field. The dinners were always over the top. At each table there would be clever toys for the guests to play with and test their creativity. One year it was building blocks . . . where we could build anything from a log cabin to a new museum! The neat thing about the blocks was that they had words engraved on them. As the evening concluded I decided to pick up a few of these blocks. The words I chose were

- Passion
- Opportunity
- Courage

These three words are a mirror of what I have tried to do with my career. *Passion* for what matters—the collections, the mission, and the people of the museum. *Opportunity*—knowing when to seize it and recognizing the people who helped me succeed. And *Courage*—to build on the opportunities, take risks, and hopefully achieve success. I believe these are traits of all successful leaders.

This book attempts to look at modern leadership theory and practice with a focus on museums. The topic is vast and this book does not attempt to cover every major leadership theory or example. As a professor of museum studies at George Washington University I developed two courses on this topic. The goal of *Leading Change in Museums* was to introduce students to for-profit and nonprofit literature and examples that provided lessons for the museum field. The class also featured case studies of leadership in museums and guest lectures by practitioners who shared their stories of change. The second course *Leading Museums in Turbulent Times* was taught on line. Here the students and I explored the reality of the many challenges and best practices in the field and how they could be prepared for their own leadership journey.

I hope this book will serve not only students but those who care deeply about museums with particular resonance to museum board members, CEOs and senior staff, consultants, volunteers, and those individuals looking to improve their leadership skills at any level. The book will also appeal to library and archives professionals, to nonprofit management students, as well as those seeking business or law degrees but with a focus on the arts and museums.

This book explores in some detail the leadership literature in for-profit and nonprofit organizations, managing change internally and externally, individual leadership traits, and approaches at many levels of the organization, current innovations in museums, and preparing the next generation. Chapters cover the context for museum leadership today including the challenges of the sector. A focus on the best practices of organizations helps to lay the groundwork for ensuing chapters on successful leaders. The chapter on organizational change covers life cycles, problems inherent in managing change, and examples of how museums are facing and coping with change.

The text further details literature on leading in contemporary society with examples of individuals who are proven models in both for profit and nonprofit settings. As leadership occurs not just at the top but at many levels, a detailed review of making change from the middle and succeeding through team-based approaches reflects this important part of the leadership continuum. Dramatic changes are occurring in all sectors of society, and museums must adopt innovative approaches involving planning, internal structure, and the interface with the external world. A chapter is devoted to new organizational designs, decision systems, and key values for assuring relevancy for museums. Today's leaders as well as the next generation must prepare through self-awareness, formal and informal training, and mentorships. The mandate for gender equality, fair pay, and diversity and inclusion are addressed as well. A substantial portion of the text is a set of nine case studies written by leaders of varied museum types and locations. Each outlines the innovative practices at their museum and several address their approach to professional development.

Throughout the text I address both business management theory and museum practice. Interviews with a variety of leaders highlight the passion and courage and thoughtful approaches of museum leaders today. To stimulate further critical thinking, each chapter includes a set of discussion questions, and the appendixes include helpful advice on learning styles and hypothetical exercises for solving common leadership challenges. A selected bibliography provides ideas for further exploration on this important topic.

ACKNOWLEDGMENTS

everal thought leaders in the museum field have made an impact on my thinking about this text. Gail Anderson, Robert R. Janes, Beth Tuttle and Anne Bergeron, Anne Ackerson and Joan Baldwin, Elaine Heumann Gurian, Gail and Barry Lord, and Marsha Semmel have all written and lectured eloquently on this topic.

Many fine examples of best practices illustrated in the book come from practitioners in the field, including Jamie O. Bosket, Michelle Delaney, Laura Huerta-Migus, Marilee Jennings, Jillian Jones, Elizabeth Kirby, Erin Mast, Jessica Nicoll, Elizabeth Pierce, Jack Rasmussen, April Salomon, Lauren Shenfeld, Sandra Smith, Lauren Telchin-Katz, and Allison Titman. Others who have contributed their ideas and experiences to my research and teaching include Harold Closter, Karen Daly, Judy Gradwohl, Julie Johnson, Nick Mann, Maureen Robinson, Kathy Dwyer Southern, Greg Stevens, and John Wetenhall. Because many of the lessons of this book reflect my teaching practice at GW Museum Studies I want to also acknowledge the support of Professor Kym Rice in encouraging me not only to pursue my courses, but in particular our mid-career leadership seminar, and of course, the writing of this text. I also owe my gratitude to Spencer Crew who as director of the National Museum of American History, gave me the opportunity to practice leadership as his deputy in the 1990s. That experience was transformative.

As always, a heartfelt thanks goes to my editor Charles Harmon and his colleagues for providing excellent feedback and guidance along the way. Finally, I owe considerable debt to my father, Thomas D. Morris, who was an amazing public servant and humble leader. His close associate Peter Drucker shared his admiration for my dad in a 1995 letter to me calling him "a model, an exemplar, and ideal of the Leader as Servant"—a high honor! I have always considered that as the model for my own career.

Martha Morris

INTRODUCTION

T his is not a book just about leadership. This is a book about public service. Leadership is a phenomenon of every sector of our lives from family to workplace to business and government. We are therefore a society obsessed with defining, criticizing, and seeking the best in leadership. There is a significant body of literature over the last century that addresses the characteristics of success for individual and organizational leadership. This literature has evolved in response to society's needs. In what are surely turbulent times, a day doesn't go by that we don't think about how to solve critical problems, how to sustain our organizations, and how to be a significant contributor to our community. Behind the fundamental obligations of preservation and stewardship of collections, museums now have responsibilities with significantly higher stakes. We have committed ourselves to contributing to the quality-of-life in our society. And we do not do this alone. We must work alongside other nonprofits, arts and cultural organizations, individual scholars and artists, and with for-profit and government bodies. Our best leaders believe in public service and citizenship, in making a difference, and upholding our values.

This book is about the context, the urgency, and the nuances of service to the mission of the museum organization whether at the level of the governing body or a middle manager. The book will therefore study the concept of followership as a necessary part of effective leadership. A focus on external and internal operations of the museum will provide a balance of perspectives. Addressing internal concerns, the book will examine organizational design, new modes of planning and decision making, implementation of strategic programs, and flexibility in the response to the reality of constant change. Externally we will look at the convergence of factors that influence success including demographic changes, political trends, globalization, and sustainability among others.

The book will highlight the leadership philosophy and literature that resonates with the challenges we face in the early twenty-first century. The voices and stories of individuals in the museum field are a featured part of this text. The importance of advocacy, persistence, creativity, and empathy will be emphasized. We need to begin by examining the challenges of museums, their staff and stakeholders.

The Leadership Challenge

Museums today face incredible challenges as well as new opportunities. Globalization, new technologies, competition, demographic change, collections preservation, accountability, financial turmoil, environmental sustainability, and staffing changes are all major concerns. We are hard at work redefining the nature of community expectations, reevaluating the composition of our boards and staff, and determining the best approaches to collections care and access. These issues are explained in more detail below.

Demographics

The aging of our workforce and population, the growth of the millennial generation, and the growing recognition of our diversity including race, gender, and ethnicity along with a growing economic divide have continued to create a complex set of challenges. This is particularly critical in the museum field as we struggle with the concept of Inclusion. These shifts also impact the visitor population and audience expectations of our museums. The reality of competition from numerous options for our leisure time or educational pursuits means that a museum visit (virtual or physical) may be less appealing to our changing populations. We compete with theaters, YouTube, amusement parks, vineyards, universities, and retail enterprise.

Technology

Growing dependence on technology in every sector allows for sharing of information and services, improved decision making, and rapid operational improvements. At the same time it places stress on the worker and leader, as the pace of change is daunting. With virtual reality will we need bricks and mortar museums? Will exhibitions be designed and built by machines? We know that younger generations are sometimes bored by museums and seek experiences that are interactive and technology-based. If we can buy everything on line and have it delivered to our door, do we need to travel to a museum? In the world of social media, will Instagram and Facebook allow for citizen curators or educators? At the same time online fundraising and marketing is increasing the number of individuals reached through the activities of crowdsourcing and crowd funding. Technology allows us to conduct business through teleconferencing, webcasts, or Skype; and, in fact, you can do your job anywhere at any time. But, this may or may not be a positive factor in making good decisions or building collaborative teams.

Globalization

Fewer trade barriers, new sources of investment, and labor in a flat world lead to a new competitive environment. Asia and the Middle East are importing our talent in building their cultural infrastructure. Their building boom leads to new competition in the art markets, the museum labor force, and pressures for possible repatriation or loan of collections to their original homelands. Along with globalization is the reality of national security in a post–9/11 world. How do we safeguard collections, facilities, staff, and visitors? Worldwide threats to cultural heritage create a new challenge for our museums already stretched thin.

Environmental Sustainability

The worldwide call for sustainability has been embraced by museums. A green imperative is evident in Leadership in Energy and Environmental Design (LEED) requirements in building construction. Museums embrace this new ethic through more flexible climate control standards, through solar power and geothermal air systems, low flow toilets, and intensive recycling. Not only do museums need to protect the environment in their operations, but they must also now provide new levels of awareness and education about these issues to their audiences. And in some cases museums will need to take the moral high ground by rejecting the financial support of corporations that spoil the environment.

Economy, Recession, and Political Sentiment

Shrinking resources have been with us for a long time, requiring ways of working smarter. Recessions are a regular and cyclical phenomenon yet museums seem to consistently get hammered by them. Too many times do we see headlines about museum layoffs, closures, or mergers. What do our government and other funders really want from the nonprofit or arts sector? Foundation support for museums is often predicated on a particular policy initiative such as community relevance. Individual donors seek projects that match their interests, but may also want to have a level of control over the outcome. Federal money has been set aside for partnerships between museums and libraries and in support of underserved communities such as tribal museums. But frequently we see pushback to shrink the federal support for arts and humanities.

The social and economic context of modern museums has spawned new efforts for change. We now see growth of grassroots advocates representative of varying communities. Museums seek economic sustainability through new business models. These may take the form of increasing revenue producing activities or corporate sponsorships. Possibly even moving into the business of consulting through providing expertise for a fee to other museums worldwide. Internally, we redefine our work processes to reengineer core processes to streamline and speed up work; or we simply outsource the work to contractors. Museums look to the for-profit sector to adopt approaches that will assure sustainability. As we move in these new directions the public reacts by demanding accountability and transparency. Are we true to our mission?

In responding to these challenges we need to face the reality of leadership failure. In cases where we are not prepared to deal with new demands we can stumble. A factor that increases this reality is that nonprofits and museums are led by volunteers. Board members are legally responsible for managing their organizations, but often are not experienced in running them effectively. We unfortunately see mismanagement and failure in our sector as a result.

Evolving demographic shifts require succession planning for retiring leaders and other key staff. Twenty-first century learning skills are the foundation of the new workforce: critical thinking, collaboration, creativity, and innovation are needed to assure museums' ability to remain sustainable and provide needed service to society.

Expansionism

The challenges of museums today involve many risks including those related to ambitious programs meant to improve the museum's reputation, attract audiences and new sources of funding. In the past two decades we have seen a building boom that has resulted in spectacular new buildings or renovated spaces in support of improved collections care, exhibitions, community events, and retail activities. As noted in the writings of Richard Florida, cities are now seeking to attract a "creative class." These artists, teachers, writers, and performers among others seek each other out and in turn create an environment that attracts new business and populations, including tourists.[1] In 2016 the *Art Newspaper* reported that this building boom represents an investment of close to five billion dollars.[2] The results are increasing audiences and operating costs, along with donor fatigue and staff burnout. Similar findings were reported in the landmark 2012 study *Set in Stone* by the University of Chicago's Cultural Policy Center.[3] That study of new art museums and performing arts centers in the US revealed that projects span close to a decade of work and frequently run over budget. A glaring example is the February 2017 resignation of the Director of New York's Metropolitan Museum of Art after implementing a costly expansion program and other new areas of growth.[4]

The museum field is certainly in turmoil over these radical changes and resulting problems. Robert Janes writing in his landmark text *Museums in a Troubled World* expressed a deep concern about the survival of museums. He feels that we are not in touch with the expectations of society and in many ways have become irrelevant. We need to focus our role in a civil society and transform or renew ourselves into what he calls the "mindful museum."[5]

The problems Janes sees are numerous. In particular museums appear to be too concerned with a marketplace mentality and adoption of business practices. This focuses energies away from public service. A myopic mind-set allows museums to avoid needed change. The most glaring example is an emphasis on money over mission. Corporatism can be defined as adopting a corporate mentality, focused on activities that provide income.[6] This leads to a loss of independence or to a blurring of the lines between for-profit and nonprofit. This plays out in activities such as lending for-profit, deaccessioning to support operations, highly paid CEOs, and corporate underwriting and implied endorsements. Are these acceptable practices? Loss of independence will evoke public scrutiny, tighter regulations, and straying from the mission.

Unhappy Staff

Individuals working in museums are highly motivated to support the mission of the museum and safeguard professional practices despite being paid relatively low wages. The risks are high. In a turbulent world staff are often demoralized by the decisions of leaders. They are concerned about lack of voice in planning and the well-being of their collections, creative programming, and colleagues. In 2017 staff at Plimoth Plantation in Massachusetts formed a union to combat low pay, unsafe working conditions, and burnout.[7]

The constant pace of change will be examined in chapter 3, but we are reminded of a countless number of challenges in the form the American Alliance of Museums' (AAM) *Trendswatch* reports.[8] Provided through the expert research of the Center for the Future of Museums, we can examine any number of trends that impact our field. Some that are critical to leadership in a modern world include

- Issues of social justice
- Climate change and long-term sustainability
- Changing nature of the labor market
- Changing nature of organizational design
- Response to technological changes

- Challenges to nonprofit tax status
- Empathy
- Agile design

Workforce Issues

How do we deal with the many new trends and the challenges of museum work in the twenty-first century? Staff are aging and lacking in the diversity that reflects our communities. Additionally, a modern world requires a more flexible and humane approach to managing people. A study conducted by the Arts Alliance of Great Britain called for a more diverse and flexible workforce, creation of new approaches to learning and training, and a new emphasis on expanded skill sets including business, leadership, and all things digital. Aside from these new workforce skills, the study recognized the need for creating organizations that are more flexible, agile, and entrepreneurial.[9] Further studies point to similar concerns for our workforce. A joint survey by the American Association for State and Local History (AASLH) and other historical associations revealed that public historians entering the field need to be "adaptable, creative, and resourceful. Concerns about decreasing public support, competition for funding, and skepticism about the value of history among some demographic groups suggest that the current generation will need to demonstrate the relevance of history and secure resources."[10]

Clearly professional standards and ethical mandates continue to evolve. Museums need highly trained staff, committed governance, and innovative leaders to assure their long-term success.

What Do Museum Leaders Need to Succeed?

In surveys conducted by the author in 2012 museum leaders and staff highlighted the importance of the following skills to effectively do their jobs or lead their organizations:[11]

- Communications
- Project management
- Interpersonal skills
- Managing change

- Fundraising
- Finance and budget
- Time management

The survey further defined that in the future museum professionals will need to be prepared to be excellent strategic planners, technology gurus, marketing geniuses, and superb collaborators with a host of partners. Although these skills will be tough to obtain, we need to be prepared. The boards seeking new executive leadership have high expectations. In reviewing recent recruitment announcements for top positions in museums we find the following desired skills, many of which are similar to those above.

- Vision and expertise in leadership and management
- Work with multiple and diverse internal and external constituencies
- Passion for and commitment to community service
- Exceptional communications skills
- Financial savvy and proven fundraising skill

On a day-to-day basis the museum professional is required to handle communications, networking, leading up, transition planning, managing projects, dealing with staff burnout, breaking down silos, convincing the board of the urgency of projects, being a change agent, and setting priorities. The following chapters will provide an in-depth look at theory and practice of modern organizational and individual success, the importance of understanding the challenge of change, and the best practices employed today. Models of museum leadership, organizational design, and leading from the middle will be detailed. The needs of preparing current and future staff to respond to today's challenges will be closely examined. This book will reflect observations and experiences of current museum professionals and feature detailed case studies of successful leaders. The overriding issue is that of values. Smithsonian Secretary David Skorton writing in *Museum* Magazine posed the question "What do we value?"[12] Without a clear answer to this question museums will flounder. Skorton suggests that approaching our mission through practice of creativity, innovation, and flexibility are imperatives as we seek to be agents of social change.

Discussion Questions

1. What current and future challenges are of concern to your museum?
2. Are the concerns and warnings defined by Robert Janes relevant today?
3. Which leadership skills are most important in the next five years?

Notes

1. Richard Florida, *The Rise of the Creative Class* (New York: Basic Books, 2002). Florida recently indicated that the growth phenomenon resulted in driving artists out of neighborhoods they can no longer afford to inhabit.

2. Julia Halperin, "US Museums Spent $5bn to Expand as Economy Shrank," *Art Newspaper*, April 4, 2016, http://theartnewspaper.com/news/us-museums-spent-5bn-to-expand-as-economy-shrank/.

3. Cultural Policy Center, *Set in Stone*, University of Chicago, 2012, http://culturalpolicy.uchicago.edu/sites/culturalpolicy.uchicago.edu/files/setinstone/index.shtml.

4. Robin Pogrebin, "Metropolitan Museum Director Resigns Under Pressure," *New York Times*, February 28, 2017, https://www.nytimes.com/2017/02/28/arts/design/met-museum-director-resigns-thomas-campbell.html?_r=0.

5. Robert Janes, *Museums in a Troubled World* (New York: Routledge, 2009), 13–25.

6. Ibid., 94–107.

7. Emily Clark, "Workers Unionize, Demand Contract," Wickedlocal.com, August 25, 2017, http://plymouth.wickedlocal.com/news/20170825/plimoth-plantation-workers-unionize-demand-contract.

8. *Trendswatch* reports have been published since 2012. The Center for the Future of Museums research provides examples of how museums adapt to these various trends. See http://aam-us.org/resources/center-for-the-future-of-museums/projects-and-reports/trendswatch.

9. Arts Council of Great Britain, "Character Matters: Attitudes, Behaviours and Skills in the Museum Workforce," September 2016, http://www.artscouncil.org.uk/sites/default/files/download-file/ACE_Museums_Workforce_ABS_BOP_Final_Report.pdf.

10. Phillip Scarpino and Daniel Vivian, "What Do Public History Employers Want?" Joint Taskforce of AASLH-AHA-NCPH-OAH study, 2015, http://ncph.org/history-at-work/report-public-history-education-and-employment/.

11. Author surveys of Museum Studies graduates, individuals working at Smithsonian Affiliates museums, and other museum listserv members, 2012.

12. David J Skorton, "What Do We Value?" *Museum* (May–June 2016): 38–43.

ORGANIZATIONAL LEADERSHIP DEFINED

Organizations are complex entities. Whether non-profit or for-profit, there are certain key character-istics that define success. This chapter will cover the research of leading business theorists regarding factors that lead to success in the modern organization. We will also examine the best practices as defined in recent literature on nonprofits including muse-ums. The important role of governance will be examined.

Business Leadership Theory

Although there are a multitude of publications on this topic, the work of Jim Collins has been widely respected for the past twenty years. He wrote a tremendously popular book in the mid-1990s—*Built to Last*—and a follow-up study titled *Good to Great*. Each continues to be very popular must-reads in the business field. Museum leaders have defi-nitely taken many of these lessons to heart, especially in the last fifteen years as we have faced many challenges in sustainability and reinven-tion. Collins based his books on extensive research about successful companies. A review of the findings of this research will help to define what effective companies look like with long-term track records.

Built to Last illustrates one of the most important factors in planning for success: benchmarking. In fact Collins's research is based on studying corporations which have been successful over a long period of time, and distilling the factors that have led to their success.[1] Benchmarking is a critical practice for all organizations going through strategic planning and transformational change. For example it involves understanding the competition, and considering what practices one might adopt to improve their chances of success such as new processes, structures, financial models, partnerships, and the like.

Working with colleague Jerry Porras at Stanford University, Collins studied twenty companies with a strong vision and record of success. These companies had been in business for a minimum of fifty years, had multiple generations of CEOs, gone through multiple life cycles, and were considered the best in their field. Well-known entities such as General Electric, IBM, Disney, and Ford were in the cohort. Factors that created their sustained success include the following

- Adherence to a set of core values
- Ability to adapt in response to a changing world
- Attention to succession planning
- Creation of internal alignment

The findings were surprising in that many of these organizations were not known for their rock star leaders, but for incremental change and innovation over time, recognition of employee contributions, and clearly articulated mission statements. These organizations would "preserve the core and stimulate progress" by being self-critical and encouraging experimentation, while protecting their core values. In regard to growth, the companies would develop "BHAGS" (Big Hairy Audacious Goals) to motivate change. Some of these organizations were considered cult-like in their discipline and passion for the mission. In addition they believed in homegrown management frequently providing intensive leadership development for their employees. Despite having ambitious sometimes risky goals that energize the workforce, there was still an adherence to tested values.

The importance of succession planning is critical in these organizations. At GE there is a process of training and weeding out the best managers. Legendary GE CEO Jack Welch paid personal attention to this process, grooming his successor for many years. Certainly it makes sense to grow management. If you invest in training and building talented staff with a belief in the core ideology, one can assume there will be long-term sustainability. And this in turn will reinforce the power of alignment behind critical goals. Organizations that are not "built to last" will likely be challenged by disarray and levels of failure.

Collins next did research looking at companies that had gone from "good to great."[2] A research team spent five years looking at several measures to assess success including organizations with at least fifteen years of financial growth. These organizations built success on a number of factors

- Being the best in the world in your core business
- Getting the right people on the bus
- Confronting data that revealed weaknesses
- Creating a culture of discipline
- Using technology as an accelerator

Collins also focused on the characteristics of the leadership of these companies. On a continuum of five levels from modest to exemplary leadership, Level 5 is characterized by personal humility and professional will. This includes a willingness to reflect success back on the workforce, not oneself. Should failure occur the Level 5 leader will accept blame. This somewhat "egoless" approach has gained considerable credibility in modern organizational theory.

Beyond this critical leadership trait, the great companies in this study had several other characteristics. Assuring that they had "the right people on the bus" exhibits a focus on hiring a strong and dedicated team. Individual character trumps a fancy resume. These organizations will provide opportunities to the best staff, while quickly removing the non-performers. Another important factor is that internal communications and decision systems are based on rigorous assessment of data. Managers lead with questions encouraging open dialogue and debate. Problems are dealt with directly. Once a team is at work there are efforts to define core competencies and refine goals. Open dialogue allows for exploration of new ideas. Yet there needs to be a balance between freedom and responsibility. In the end, success is predicated on discipline. For example, in strategic planning the organization may have many worthy and exciting options. But hard decisions based on facts will lead to a small number of priorities or even a list of activities that will no longer be supported. The concepts in this book rely on the value of technology in reaching new markets as well as supporting back of house operations.

How does any of this thinking impact the museum world? In 2005 Collins was inspired to look more closely at the nonprofit sector in his monograph *Good to Great and the Social Sectors*.[3] This was not based on extensive research of nonprofits but his analysis of the field was helpful. He stated that

- You don't have to be like a business to succeed, but you do need discipline
- Measuring impact is critical to assess your ability to achieve mission

Collins believes that Level 5 leaders are especially effective in the social sectors.[4] The power of inclusion and coalition building is critical to a complex governance and diffuse power structure that is typical of the nonprofit world. Consider professional staff, boards, and audiences and the need to create leaders who will listen and collaborate on goals. Collins recognizes the difficulty of attracting workers who are subject to low pay. So motivating them with the mission is critical. Successful nonprofits can build the organization's brand, manage cash flow, secure services of volunteers, and build on strength in creating projects that will accelerate growth and support the community.[5] Interestingly enough this community focus is not singular to nonprofits. For example, see Starbucks' published core values below.[6]

- Creating a culture of warmth and belonging, where everyone is welcome.
- Acting with courage, challenging the status quo and finding new ways to grow our company and each other.
- Being present, connecting with transparency, dignity and respect.
- Delivering our very best in all we do, holding ourselves accountable for results.
- We are performance driven, through the lens of humanity.

Beyond a commitment to mission, values, and community, successful organizations also are characterized by "open book management" and a "fair process" in decision making. The former relies heavily on practices of sharing information widely with staff. An organization that relies on internal learning and transparency in operations is clearly ahead of the game.[7] The open book approach is one where the company's operating information is available to staff in the process of planning and evaluation. This sharing allows for better understanding of product outcomes, budget realities, and customer views. The more knowledgeable the staff members are, the better decisions they make. In a similar vein, a "Fair Process" as outlined by Kim and Mauborgne in the late 1990s promotes a collaborative approach to decisions about future directions, through three steps: Engagement, Explanation, and Expectations Clarity. Achieving buy-in and building trust require that leaders establish a process that seeks wide feedback in deliberation on strategic decisions, that clearly justifies the option selected, and finally lays out the required actions for individual employees.[8]

Probably learning from the intrinsic value of the nonprofit sector, many corporations are now openly seeking opportunities to make a difference. In their landmark essay on "Creating Shared Value," Harvard professors Michael Porter and Mark Kramer advocated for a public service collaboration between for-profit, the social sectors, and government.[9] Although it is a new way of thinking for the museum field, there could be exceptional synergy in working in tandem with the for-profit sector to deliver on mission. Socially motivated businesses focus on issues of worker treatment, sustainable practices, responsible manufacturing, and actively contribute funds to social causes. The question is one of blurring boundaries and associating the mission driven nonprofit with a for-profit organization. These innovative models will be explored in greater detail in chapter 6.

Nonprofit Board Governance

A study published in *Harvard Business Review* in 2015 revealed that nonprofit boards fell short in several critical areas: understanding the organization's mission, lacking a succession plan for the CEO/ executive director, feeling overwhelmed by fundraising duties, and experiencing frequent upheaval in governance.[10] We know the challenges of leadership of the nonprofit sector in general and the museum sector in particular as outlined in chapter 1. An example of governance in upheaval is the crisis that faced the Smithsonian Institution from 2007 through 2009 when a complete leadership overhaul was required after their board failed to recognize top-level financial mismanagement.[11] In this case, the world's largest and most respected museum system was subject to congressional investigation over top leadership abuses of power. This resulted in a complete overhaul of the board of regents' bylaws, structure, and key leadership roles. A new code of ethics and a performance tracking system was published on their website to allow for greater transparency in resolution of problems.[12] A similar problem occurred at the Los Angeles County Museum of Contemporary Art where mismanagement of assets led the California state attorney general to order the board to undergo training in financial management.[13]

It appears these two museums and likely several others were not familiar with or practicing established nonprofit board best practices. The 1996 landmark work by Taylor, Chait, and Holland[14] outlines a variety of approaches that empower boards to be more proactive and effective including

- Collaborating closely with the CEO
- Being issues-oriented, not process driven
- Being analytical problem-solvers
- Being diverse in skills and demographics
- Operating with trust, respect, and candor
- Seeking out information from varied sources
- Setting performance measures

There are many dynamics to an effective board. In 2017 the American Alliance of Museums and BoardSource partnered on a new initiative for improving board performance.[15] The findings of *Museum Board Leadership 2017: A National Report* were based on a survey with 1,600 responses from all sectors of the field. Both board chairs and CEOs responded. The survey revealed a lack of diversity in board membership, an emphasis on the role of fundraising, an alarming lack of focus on advocacy, and little or no effort at self-assessment. Performance goals were lacking as well as consistent approaches to succession planning for the CEO position. On a positive note the relationship between CEO and board chair was reported as largely positive. Board culture received lower marks in the area of attendance and in the lower percentage of focus on strategic issues and taking responsibility for failures. In an era of increasing pressure on nonprofits to prove that they are a fundamental part of the social fabric and economic vitality of the nation the AAM is now taking steps with this initiative to give boards and CEOs an opportunity to develop best practices for engaging communities and legislators.[16] Further board development programs will be a strategic initiative of the AAM going forward. Fortunately some museum boards are taking action already. An important factor in measuring success is developing performance metrics, and a good example of this is the work of the Speed Museum in Louisville, Kentucky. Their board has developed a dashboard for assuring that their membership is truly diverse.[17]

Museum Standards and Best Practices

Underlying the success of this new governance effort are the fundamentals of the AAM assessment and accreditation program that assure our ability to secure the public trust.[18] Textbox 2.1 outlines the areas that responsible leaders need to address.

Overall the field has adopted a set of common practices over the past several decades. All museums need to adhere to these basic ten-

---

Textbox 2.1.
ASSURING PUBLIC TRUST

A Clear Mission and Articulated Values
Adherence to a Code of Ethics
Accountability through Performance Measures
Financial Stability
Collections and Facilities Care
Attention to Human Resource Management
Transparency in Policies and Decision Making
Community Impact
Strong Leadership

ants that emphasize stewardship, public service, transparency, and prohibit conflicts of interest. Museum ethics codes cover many areas including collections acquisition, lending and borrowing, working with businesses and individual donors, governing transparently, deaccessioning, and repatriation to name a few. Similar statements have been developed by the American Association for State and Local History, International Council of Museums, and the Association of Art Museum Directors. Probably the most rigorous approach to codifying best practices is the process of accreditation administered by the American Alliance of Museums. This is a peer review system, awarded to a small fraction of the museums in the United States. Fortunately, there is nothing stopping a museum from adopting the published best practices of the accreditable museum.

Looking at textbox 2.2 the basic AAM standards are listed on the left while the best practices are listed on the right. For example, in the area of planning, a museum should have a current strategic plan, while in regard to facilities green approaches to sustainability are the best practice. Probably one of the most important activities is making sound decisions. Museums must avoid major risks in managing collections, staff, funds, and facilities. The basis for decision making is a strategic plan (see figure 2.1).

Museum planning starts with an environmental analysis. The Strengths, Weaknesses, Opportunities and Threats (SWOT) approach leads to a defined vision of success for the future and aligns itself with the museum's mission statement. Goals and action plans are ways of

---

Textbox 2.2.
STANDARDS AND BEST PRACTICES

Standards	Best Practices
Planning	Strategic Plan
Collections	Collecting Plan
Ethics	Transparency in Decisions
Fundraising	Donor/sponsor policies
Facilities	Green Design
Finance	Balanced sources
Staffing	Staff Development
Governance	Board/CEO Relations

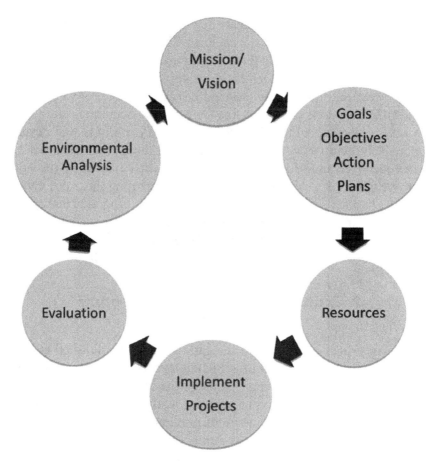

Figure 2.1. Strategic planning process.
Courtesy of the author.

defining the deliverable projects that will achieve the vision. For example, an important goal is the development of a collecting plan to guide future acquisitions and decisions. Museums can have many goals and even more objectives. The trick is to set priorities, sequences, and test for viability. As plans become more concrete, resources can be allocated, such as staff time or funds. Of course fundraising is often the expected method of acquiring resources. Implementation of objectives can occur over a period of time and as they are completed an evaluation of their success or failure is undertaken. The lessons learned from that evaluation connect directly back into the environmental analysis. It's a circular process and there can be iterations back and forth. Plans need to be flexible and dynamic. Plans also are developed and reviewed by groups of staff, board, and external stakeholders. The standard today includes a set of operating values that form a framework for decisions. An excellent example of this approach is the strategic plan created by the San Diego Museum of Man. The museum has adopted a set of values that guide their key decisions and define their internal operating culture.[19]

One strategic goal that is becoming a high priority is staff development. Individuals need to be given growth opportunities, learn to work effectively in the organization, and be poised to move up the ladder. We will look at how museums are implementing these programs in later chapters. The best examples include those programs that assist staff in communications, team learning, project management, time management, dealing with change, and executive coaching. And training in customer service and audience sensitivity is also important.

A Snapshot of Twenty-First-Century Museum Models

A research study conducted in the early 2000s and published by the American Alliance of Museums highlights a set of six case studies reflecting successful museums. Although the criteria are not as extensive as those defined by Collins et al. above, they do represent a more systematic approach to evaluation of museum success. *Magnetic, The Art and Science of Engagement* by Anne Bergeron and Beth Tuttle features selected museums that exhibited best practices in financial stability and public service. Benchmarks included an analysis of quantitative and qualitative measures: annual attendance, operating budget, revenue sources, membership, number of staff, endowment, and programs over a ten-year period to gauge their sustainability (1999–2009). Several other factors were examined including mission, values, leadership, community building, visitor engagement, marketing, and branding. Important success factors included alignment of all stakeholders both inside and outside the organization, emphasis on customer service, building relationships, and innovative programs.[20] Museums featured in the text include the Children's Museum of Pittsburgh and their incubator programs for neighborhood youth; the Chrysler Museum and a philosophy that encourages everyone on staff to be a leader; the Conner Prairie Museum's innovative visitor engagement programs; the

Franklin Institute and its magnet high school for STEM (Science, Technology, Engineering and Mathematics) learning; and the Philbrook Museum of Art's twenty or more immersive community partnerships.[21] In summary these organizations succeed by valuing the following:[22]

- Human and intellectual resources
- Social capital among stakeholders
- Building on good will and reputation
- Financial stability

One area that has grown in importance as a best practice in the museum field is that of data metrics. Museums that are cautious in their stewardship of human and financial resources will rely heavily on data associated with audiences and financial performance. Responding to this need are organizations such as the Association of Science and Technology Centers, the Association of Children's Museums, and the American Zoological Association. These provide benchmarks for their members. Individual museums are increasingly developing their own metrics related to strategic goals. And the smart practice is now to build financial literacy in all staff.[23]

The following chapters will give the reader a chance to learn about a variety of successful museums, their ability to transform themselves to meet the challenges of the twenty-first-century world, and the nature and character of the individuals who have led these efforts. The next chapter will look at the process of leading change in organizations and the hurdles that pivotal leaders need to confront in transforming their organizations.

Discussion Questions

1. Can museums benefit from the lessons of successful businesses? Would this approach in any way compromise the ethics and independence of the museum sector?
2. How do museum boards become more accountable and reinvent themselves according to the best practices in nonprofit governance?
3. In thinking about Jim Collins's ideas about Level 5 leadership, which museum leaders might exemplify these traits?
4. Given the characteristics of successful museums as identified by the AAM, how does your museum measure up?

Notes

1. Jim Collins and Jerry Porras, *Built to Last* (New York: HarperBusiness, 1994).

2. Jim Collins, *Good to Great* (New York: HarperCollins, 2001).

3. Jim Collins, *Good to Great and the Social Sectors* (self-published, 2005).

4. Ibid., 9–12.

5. Ibid., 32–33.

6. Starbucks, "Our Values," https://www.starbucks.com/about-us/company -information/mission-statement.

7. John Case, *Open-Book Management: The Coming Business Revolution* (New York: HarperBusiness, 1995).

8. W. Chan Kim and Renee Mauborgne, "Fair Process: Managing in the Knowledge Economy," *Harvard Business Review* 75, no. 4 (July–August 1997): 69.

9. Michael E. Porter and Mark R. Kramer, "Creating Shared Value," *Harvard Business Review* 89, nos.1–2 (January–February 2011): 62–77.

10. "The Sorry State of Nonprofit Boards," *Harvard Business Review*, September 2015, https://hbr.org/2015/09/the-sorry-state-of-nonprofit-boards.

11. Pete Smith, "Tongue Tied at the Top," in *Stanford Social Innovation Review* (Spring 2009), https://ssir.org/articles/entry/what_didnt_work_tongue _tied_at_the_top.

12. *Board of Regents Has Implemented Many Governance Reforms, but Ensuring Accountability and Oversight Will Require Ongoing Action.* Report by the Government Accountability Office, May 2000, http://www.gao.gov/ products/GAO-08-632.

13. Randy Kennedy, "Los Angeles Museum Board Members Ordered to Undergo Financial Training," *New York Times*, April 19, 2010, https://artsbeat .blogs.nytimes.com/2010/04/19/los-angeles-museum-board-members -ordered-to-undergo-financial-training/?emc=etal.

14. Barbara Taylor, Richard Chait, and Thomas Holland, "New Work of the Nonprofit Board," *Harvard Business Review* (September–October 1996), https://hbr.org/1996/09/the-new-work-of-the-nonprofit-board.

15. BoardSource, *Museum Board Leadership 2017: A National Report* (Washington, DC: BoardSource, 2017).

16. American Alliance of Museums, *Stand for Your Mission*, 2016, http:// standforyourmission.org/wp-content/uploads/2016/09/stand-for-your -mission-museum-guide.pdf.

17. Ted Loos, "Speed Turns to a Spreadsheet to Increase Diversity," *New York Times*, March 17, 2016, https://www.nytimes.com/2016/03/17/arts/design/ speed-museum-turns-to-a-spreadsheet-to-increase-diversity.html?_r=0.

18. Martha Morris, "Maintaining the Public Trust," *Newstandard* (Summer 2006): 4–5.

19. San Diego Museum of Man Strategic Plan, http://www.museumofman .org/strategicplan/.

20. Anne Bergeron and Beth Tuttle, *Magnetic: The Art and Science of Engagement* (Washington, DC: American Alliance of Museums Press, 2013), 9–10.

21. Ibid., 27.

22. Ibid., 163.

23. Anne Bergeron and Beth Tuttle, "A Magnetic Science Center," *Museum* 96, no. 3 (2017): 34.

LEADERSHIP THEORY AND MANAGING CHANGE

All **organizations** including museums go through change, and managing this challenge is critical for success. This chapter will look at how organizations evolve through a life cycle; the key elements in implementing a change effort; the problems inherent in managing change; and examples of how museums are successfully facing and coping with change. Discussion of the implications of leadership turnover, reorganization, mergers, and other disruptive factors for museums illustrate the challenge.

Change in Museums

In chapter 1 we examined a host of external factors that affect how museums must cope in the modern world. These include the shifting demographics of audiences, competition, technology, climate change, globalization, economic downturns, building expansions, and workforce demands. In particular twenty-first century concerns now include the reality of a digital civil society, increasing reliance on forms of self-governance, personalized learning, and social justice as key drivers of community responsiveness. Museums must be better advocates for their role in society. In fact we need transformational change to assure that we will remain relevant and resilient in a turbulent world. Let's examine some of these trends and how our museums are coping.

Retrenchment

In recent decades the museum field has seen the duality of rapid growth in start-ups and new building while facing significant funding cutbacks. In reaction museums have taken a variety of steps including salary and hiring freezes, converting jobs to temporary appointments, hiring contract workers, and relying more on volunteers and interns. Cyclical recessions and government cuts have led to downsizing or layoffs. Significant impacts of the Great Recession starting in 2008 led to a drop in investment income and fewer philanthropic gifts. Museums such as the Seattle Art Museum, Taubman Museum of Art, the Metropolitan Museum of Art, and the Getty all saw layoffs as a result. Often layoffs were necessitated by financial strains but sometimes these actions relate to the need to restructure staff to meet new strategic goals. For example, in 2012 the Getty laid off members of their education staff and redirected funds to curatorial and collections priorities.[1] In 2014 the Hirshhorn Museum in Washington decided to replace its long-term docent core to bring on a younger cadre of visitor services staff. Many docents had been working at the museum for up to forty years, but the museum wanted to reach a younger demographic.[2]

Sometimes these staff changes are dramatic events, such as the early 2017 downsizing Colonial Williamsburg announced without advanced warning, which affected staff in core interpretive programs. The reasoning put forward was the need to address "significant and difficult changes in relation to financial sustainability."[3] This news was followed by Washington's Newseum announcing its fifth round of layoffs since opening its new facility in 2008, this time cutting twenty-six positions.[4] Later in 2017 Colonial Williamsburg announced a new restructuring and massive layoffs to save the organization. Apparently the organization was spending down its endowment in order to bolster its failing for-profit arm.[5]

Even in the 1990s there were seeds of change at work in museums. Surveys conducted by the author found that 83 percent of responding museums were undergoing organizational change including reacting to decreased funding especially from government sources. Other reasons for change were operating new buildings, the priorities of new directors, and staff turnover. Overriding many of the change programs was the mandate to provide better service to communities. Most encouraging were signs that senior leaders wanted to implement values-based systems of decision making and inclusive practices involving staff. Internal communications became an important focus and many modes of information sharing and seeking staff input were bubbling up.[6] Changes in organizational structure and operations were frequent in the museums surveyed. The types of changes reported included moving from functional silos to program-based units, museum-wide open book management in regards to financials, new departments dedicated to fundraising and technology, and a focus on customer relations.

Collections at Risk

Heritage Preservation studies in 2004 and later revealed large numbers of collections were uncataloged, poorly housed, or in need of basic stabilization treatment.[7] Museum capacity to care for collections is lagging and may lead to active deaccessioning. For example the Brooklyn Museum transferred textile and costume items to the Metropolitan Museum in 2009.[8] Despite the growing burden of collections management and care, many museums still fail in creating collecting plans to guide future acquisitions. Further concerns arise about portions of collections becoming "orphaned" due to the retirement of long-term staff in key curatorial or other collections specialties. In fact museums have consciously directed their sparse resources to public activities such as educational programs, exhibitions, web programs, new buildings, as well as fundraising and marketing. Often this is at the expense of collections care. Not only are collections at risk but also museum facilities continue to face backlogs of deferred maintenance. The Smithsonian Institution reported a striking one-billion-dollar backlog in facilities projects in the spring of 2017.

Leadership Turnover

As reported in the *Art Newspaper* there are a growing number of vacant director positions in the United States (and likely in other countries).[9] Turnover of retiring directors can result in numerous openings, lags in hiring, and levels of uncertainty on the part of the staff. Practically every major city, region in the country, and type of museum has seen this phenomenon. As positions are filled with new directors, opportunities for change abound. Each new director will likely want to change the organizational structure—and in many cases create a new strategic plan. A case in point is the new direction outlined by Smithsonian secretary David Skorton in 2017. Building on the work of the previous secretary's comprehensive plan, Skorton added new areas of emphasis and strategies meant to strengthen the online presence of the institution, as well as diversify revenue in an era of Congressional cutbacks. As the plan rolled out, all of the programmatic (museum) and support (administrative) offices worked on ways to develop complimentary plans to implement the new vision. For example, with a renewed emphasis on civic engagement, new audiences will need to be reached through educational programs, digital connections, and collaborations with external groups. A focus on "One Smithsonian" underscores the need to create cross-functional planning groups, shared resources, and new operational policies and standards critical in a time of fiscal restraint.[10] New strategic plans are one example, but often new directors need to move quickly to respond to external changes, particularly audience demands. The more traditional the museum the more difficult this is. If you have a large encyclopedic collection with significant facility overhead it may be difficult to swiftly change course and build new collections and exhibitions that focus on contemporary art, for example. The impact on established programs and the work of staff will be disruptive.

All leadership changes bring with them a period of adjustment. The transfer of power in government, industry, and nonprofits is always a time of stress for those impacted. It raises the question of the type of leader needed for the organization and its relative stability. Do we need strong leaders who can turn around a failing organization? Do we need a leader who can make incremental change to meet external expectations and challenges? Do we need a radical redesign of our systems and programs? Or do we need a leader who will sustain the status quo? What are the characteristics we are looking for in a good leader? Why are people so disappointed with our presidents, executives of nonprofits, and corporate leaders? As public citizens, community members, customers, shareholders, or staff members how do we adjust to new operating styles, policy mandates, organizational restructuring, and distribution of power? With every change in an organization, be it consolidations, new partnerships, or bankruptcies, there is going to be a huge impact on the way those organizations do business.

Change can be viewed positively or negatively depending on your situation. When Secretary Larry Small left the Smithsonian in 2007 there were probably staff who saw that as positive, while others saw the negative. Positive because they didn't think he was doing a good job; negative because their own jobs might have been in jeopardy. The reality of constant turnover in a museum can be extremely disruptive. The Please Touch Museum in Philadelphia has had several directors since moving to its new building in 2008. Likewise, the Historical Society of Washington, DC, has had several directors since moving to a new facility in 2001. Every time a new director comes on board there are start-up challenges. The adjustments for staff can be substantial. Interim directors may step in to sustain the organization while a new executive is sought. Sometimes museum boards look for non-traditional candidates who may have business skills but know little about nonprofits and museums.

As mentioned above in this period of new leadership or even under an existing leader the museum may seek to restructure to better serve their mission and public. Or in a more dire situation a merger with another museum may be the answer. The reorganization is almost always in service of the mission in that key staff needs to be in place to implement new programs. Restructuring may also be needed if a significant downsizing occurs and program units need to be combined. The reality is that these structural adjustments are made on a fairly frequent basis.

There are many reasons to implement a reorganization. The most common ones include

- Implementation of a new strategic plan
- Economic impact and downsizing
- New director

- Expansion and growth
- Staff succession and turnover
- Diversity initiatives

The Turnaround

Famous for saving several performing arts organizations, Michael Kaiser shared lessons from these turnarounds in his 2008 publication. Key strategies for success were to never cut core programs, and to invest in aggressive marketing. The importance of saving the heart or mission-related work of the nonprofit is critical as is convincing major funders that the organization is well managed and knows its weaknesses and strengths through a strategic planning process. This lesson is critical for museums that might consider an across-the-board cut or be willing to sacrifice core staff to save money. Any cuts should be strategic.[11]

Life Cycle Context

Understanding the change process is best grounded in the knowledge of where your museum is on the organizational life cycle. The life cycle illustrated (see textbox 3.1) shows six stages of growth, senility, and renewal.

With this model we can gain insight into the dynamics of change and the ability of an organization to adjust to the various phases.[12] In the early years of a new organization (Infancy and Adolescence) there is little structure, rapid growth, uncertainty, excitement and likely a dominate founder or leader. As the organization develops its plans, seeks external partners, raises money, and staffs up, there is a struggle to create a balance between growth and stability. At the level of Prime a museum should be stable enough

---

**Textbox 3.1.
MUSEUM LIFE CYCLES**

- *Infancy:* founding excitement
- *Adolescence:* rapid growth and chaos
- *Prime:* successful and improving
- *Aristocracy:* resting on laurels
- *Bureaucracy:* rules rule
- *Senility:* time for closure or rebirth

to allow for areas of growth, while creating systems that will allow for secure management. As a museum moves into Aristocracy there is a tendency to reject risk, having a sense of invulnerability due to reputation or financial assets. If a museum moves to Bureaucracy, the zeal for new ideas is dominated by rules and restrictions that can quickly lead to unhappy staff and turnover. The drop to Senility is the point where relevance is no longer possible and change is the only option if the organization is going to survive. Any museum can go back and forth in the cycle. The importance is understanding where your museum lies on this continuum. Leading change in a bureaucracy may be an effort in futility! An important concern for combating complacency is organizational culture. A dramatic example of the life cycle and change is the Metropolitan Museum of Art in New York. In 2017 the director, Thomas Campbell, resigned under pressure. Considerable changes had been implemented under his tenure including digital programs, website redesign, rebranding, and new public programming. Most influential was an emphasis on contemporary art and an expansion to a new facility. All these changes were costly and overspending became an issue. But more fundamentally, as an Aristocratic organization, the changes were implemented too quickly.[13]

Staff Reactions to Change

Managing change in times of crisis can be a delicate process for museum leaders. Elaine Gurian described the impact on staff of the Boston Children's Museum during a transition to a new facility in "Moving the Museum," an essay in her 1995 publication *Institutional Trauma*. This move involved new ways of working between staff and contractors and among the staff themselves. Staff suffered from a sense of isolation in the process and uncertainty over roles and responsibilities in a new environment, demanding much more attention from top management than had been anticipated.[14] With every change in an organization, be it reorganizations, mergers, new partnerships, bankruptcies, or new leadership there is going to be a huge impact on the way those organizations do business. On a personal level staff members will be worried about

- Will people lose their jobs?
- Will they be asked to move?

- Will they have new responsibilities?
- Who will be in power?

In the author's experience the following statements were reactions to the reorganization planned at the National Museum of American History in 1995:

"Change is good as long as I don't need to participate."
"Change is good as long as there are no surprises."

Why is change so difficult? Individuals react differently depending on a number of factors including their learning styles, their status in the organization, and their professional expectations. Unfortunately in a change program there is certainty that staff will present management with a variety of reactions as listed in textbox 3.2.

These reactions are largely negative and can persist through the change process without proper intervention. An example is the reorganization occurring under a new leader. An article in the *New York Times* from July 1999 discussed the trend of museum restructuring interviewing curators who were fearful of depart-

> **Textbox 3.2.**
> **STAFF REACTIONS**
> **TO CHANGE**
>
> - Confusion
> - Withdrawal
> - Anger and Resistance
> - Loss of Identity

ment mergers, new support departments, and a centralization of power that "devalues" the curator. Underlying this sentiment was alarm that the museum was shifting to "business practices" that favored fundraising and marketing.[15] This trend took off in the early 1990s and continues today. An organizational change creates a dissonance that leads to loss of control, a change in status, and the potential of losing positive working relationships. However, some individuals may react more positively, seeing the change as an opportunity for growth and improvement.

Underlying the change process is the issue of a compact between the employee and management. This compact has three levels. The formal relationship with the organization includes the job description and performance expectations. The psychological compact is an implicit relationship based on trust. The social compact relates to how management behaves in regard to its stated values. Each of these three elements can be impacted by change. The social and psychological levels are often most at risk in a change effort.[16] Change is usually beneficial for the growth of the organization, but how do you introduce it in such a way as to ameliorate the concerns of staff? At a minimum it is important to share how any change will impact the individual's formal contract, or day-to-day work. Moreover, individuals need to know what they can do to implement the change.

Ways of Coping

The best approach is to assist staff in understanding the change period as a transitional one. Often there is a spirit of experimentation and creativity. Management should also be frank about not having all the answers. Finally, treating the past with respect helps to ease the transition phase. For example, in the case of moving to a new facility there is value in celebrating the past, honoring what the old facility meant for the staff, and making this an opportunity to bring everyone together, including the board. The George Washington University Museum did this when they merged with the Textile Museum in 2015.

The transitional phase of a change effort has been written about extensively, and the work of William Bridges is a classic. He describes three phases: (1) Endings and announcing the change, (2) the Neutral Zone where individuals work on new ideas, and (3) New Beginnings where staff are ready to move forward in the new environment. Any of the phases can stall the process. Individuals realize the old structures and ways of doing business are no longer acceptable, that there are still unanswered questions about the new plan, and yet individuals will be ready to move on at different times in the process. The "Neutral Zone" is where flux and uncertainly are prevalent and many people are uncomfortable. Underlying a successful change process are the following.[17]

- Communications
- Consistent behavior
- Dealing with resistance

Surveys conducted by the author revealed that museums undergoing changes provided support to their staff in several ways including counseling, coaching, intensive communications, celebrations, and above all, patience. The National Museum of American History implemented a new strategic plan and reorganization in 1995.[18] Over 50 percent of the staff participated in the strategic planning effort with close attention to staff ideas of bottom up planning. The reorganization that resulted in the implementation phase of the plan was dramatic. Over twenty separate curatorial offices were combined into eight renamed divisions; staff moved to new office clusters; new managers were appointed to run various programs; and major functional units were renamed. Several steps were taken to assure a smooth transition. First the director appointed a staff task force to develop a set of three options for the reorganization. Their deliberations were widely shared with all staff. After the director selected a plan and assigned key associate directors, the process of reorganization was underway. A period of six months was designated to be a transition period. To facilitate this a staff-driven transition working group was formed. Membership was self-selected and no managers were allowed to sit on this group. Their mandate was to work with staff throughout the organization to provide feedback to management on the progress of reorganization. Other activities implemented in this process included optional change management workshops, supervisory, teambuilding and communications training, town hall meetings, suggestion boxes, and brown bag lunch sessions with the director. Finally an employee assistance office was available for counseling staff.

Another more dramatic practice that involves a major change for museums is the merger. In these cases it is likely that layoffs will occur. Mergers have distinct legal implications and can have lasting impacts. There is always risk as well as reward. Museums are attracted to this option by various benefits such as economies of scale; savings in administrative overhead; access to donors, members, facilities, talented staff and significant collections; and improved community relations. Yet risks abound, including confusion about brand image, leadership changes and staff layoffs, board struggles, unclear expectations, canceled projects, and delays in AAM accreditation. Community feelings can run deep, as many museums have a long history of service and respect. Merging requires careful financial planning, feasibility studies, and good communication. It is also a lengthy process, sometimes unfolding over years. Most mergers are motivated by the need for survival. A case study is that of the Cincinnati Museum Center (CMC) created from a merger of three entities in the 1990s. The Children's Museum, Natural History and Science, and History Museum merged over a number of years and occupied a new facility, the landmark Union Terminal. The process involved creating one board, a single vision for the organization, and blending of staff. After several years of struggle, the museum eventually succeeded under the leadership of Douglass McDonald who also developed a new strategic plan and business model. As a result of this successful merger, the CMC merged with another local museum, the National Underground Railroad Museum and Freedom Center in 2012. Lessons learned for successful mergers include the importance of a strong leader, creating an integration plan, and practicing transparent decision making.[19] Despite these factors there are many hurdles to overcome in a major change process such as a reorganization or merger. More often the merger results in layoffs. Although these are usually formal and often legal issues, there are many ways to make the process less painful. The organization is not obligated to provide a reason for an individual layoff; still there is a moral obligation to treat these staff with respect. It is important to avoid a situation where the individual feels they have done something wrong. And they should be thanked for their service.

Change Leadership Theory

Understanding the basics of successfully managing changes such as mergers and reorganizations requires an examination of best practices in business literature. Probably the most well-known model is that espoused by John Kotter, emeritus professor at Harvard Business School. Like the work of Jim Collins, Kotter's research and writing are widely respected. His landmark book *Leading Change*, 1996, has spawned an international consulting business. Nonprofits can take lessons from this management approach.[20]

Kotter has defined eight stages of change (see figure 3.1). One could argue that these stages are somewhat repetitive but all have value. Setting the stage Kotter defines problems in organizations that fail to accept change including complacency, lack of vision, poor communications, and backsliding. Therefore there is a need to establish a *sense of urgency* early in the process. This is hugely important because

Figure 3.1. Kotter leading change.
Courtesy kotterinternational.com.

complacency and inability to get problems on the table will be a road-block. Organizations tend to deny the fact that there is a problem, and commonly revert to what Kotter calls "happy talk." Considering an organization's place on the life cycle (see textbox 3.1) there is likely going to be trouble in facing reality. Kotter sees this as such a critical phase that he notes that management will not move forward without a visible crisis. He observes that managers tend to spend a lot of time just debating, not taking action. This occurs in organizations like museums, which are academically oriented and love to debate the issues. But providing a lot of information about the problems and creating the outsized goals to push people forward is what is important. Hard data about the state of the organization is critical in making the case for a major change effort. For example if a layoff is required, there should be clear explanations of the financial situation and the options senior management considered to avoid job losses. Often at this stage it is middle management or lower levels in the museum that raises red flags. A famous incident is that of the National Zoo, which suffered from poor animal care practices in the early 2000s. The red flags were raised in that case by the registrar.

Once the organization has accepted the need for change, it must create a guiding coalition. Because decisions are complex and need to be made quickly, the coalition should include individuals with position power, credibility, and expertise. Having well-respected staff members on this team is critical. Individuals in the organization who can serve as "change agents" will provide credibility. Kotter warns to avoid *egos* and *snakes* on the team. As with any high-performing team the organization needs a group that works on trust and a common goal. Avoiding power struggles is important. Do not let a big ego dominate the team. A snake will undermine the change process. They say yes in a meeting but behind your back they are very critical.

Setting vision will provide the power to break through resistance and build alignment. Kotter expects that vision must be feasible, desirable, and clear; and at the same time be a stretch goal. This is often the most difficult part of the process. How do you create a vision that people will get behind? Will your museum be the best at providing inclusive programming? Will your community be a part of the planning? Will your collections management systems be improved? A vision should be descriptive of a positive future state.

Communicating the vision requires clear and consistent messaging. It is important to keep it simple, repeat it frequently, use stories of how the vision will be implemented, put money behind it, and listen to feedback. The American Alliance of Museums rolled out a new strategic plan via social media and a listening tour. As diversity is a critical plank in their plan, a full-time staff position was created to advocate for and implement this program. Implementing the vision also means *empowering staff* to overcome barriers to change. Often this means reorganizing, changing policy and process, training individuals, and confronting naysayers at all levels.

Kotter advocates for quickly seeking *short-term wins*. When staff see that something positive has occurred it extinguishes naysayers, builds momentum, and encourages buy in. If your change is important enough to attract an investment from a major funder, for example, then staff will understand the value. *Consolidating gains* requires diligence in pushing forward with change. Resistance is waiting for you! Keep up the momentum. The forward progress can also impact existing operations. If funding comes to support your educational programs, how will this require staff to alter established methods? What new problems could arise? For example, a new building project may help draw in new audiences but could create problems with collections preservation. So all elements must change in tandem and that is very hard to do.

Eventually the change process will take hold across the organization. *Wide-scale change* allows the entire organization to embrace the new direction and eventually results in embedding the new vision in the organizational culture. Shared values and new approaches do not happen overnight. And the change process can be derailed by many factors including leadership turnover, economic downturns, or poor planning.

In the museum field the work of Robert Janes and his staff at the Glenbow Museum has fortunately been well documented. The steps that Kotter recommends were not used as a guideline, but the Glenbow case study reflects some of these same ideas, in particular the sense of urgency when the museum was facing dramatic cuts from the federal government in the early 1990s. A clear vision for change was developed in six strategies implemented through a radical reorganization of staff functions. Working over a decade with staff, Janes created a strategic plan, built an operating endowment, culled their collections through mission-driven deaccessioning, flattened the organizational structure, and embraced their community in programming.[21] Similarly the organizational change that occurred at the National Museum of American History throughout the early part of the twenty-first century also involved reacting to the needs of a changing world, responding to new communities, and building on the strengths of the museum's collections and scholarship. The change process was led by a guiding coalition of staff from all levels of the organization, involved museum-wide involvement in creating their initial strategic plan in 1994, and led to a new and more efficient organizational structure. Based on a culture of collaboration with staff, leadership, and board, the museum was successful in facing three leadership changes between 2001 and 2008 and in implementing two successful strategic plans. The external world and the complexity of managing organizations led to both leadership turnover and the need to adapt our organizations to the reality of disruptive change in society.[22]

Looking at the art museum field there are a number of interesting examples of leading change. Brian Ferriso, in his role as a new director at the Portland Art Museum, led what he describes as an incremental change process. As an aristocracy the museum was in need of many changes as they recovered from a major expansion. Deficit spending was one such factor. Ferriso's vision for change was to focus on the collections, on improving accessibility, and on instituting fiscal responsibility. His cautious approach to working with staff and community as well as improved transparency were important to stabilizing the organization.[23]

Another example of a successful reorganization under a new leader and a new strategic plan is the Toledo Museum of Art. In 2010 director Brian Kennedy led an effort to create a new strategic plan to shore up their financial situation among other goals. The process included the voices of over 400 individuals and led to a four-year plan with a clear and compelling mission, vision, and goals. Central to the process was a restructuring that would build on the museum's strengths. One goal was to build a twenty-first-century organization that would include "innovative management and fundraising practices." The structural changes implemented in 2013 emphasized a matrix approach that would assign key strategies to cross-functional teams. Members of senior leadership were assigned as "sponsors" of the major strategies. As often happens in reorganizations there were some staff departures and new hires. At the same time the museum has focused on priority programs and giving staff an opportunity to implement innovative ideas and grow professionally.[24]

Another example of a museum undergoing significant culture change is the Minnesota Historical Society. They are leading an effort both internally and field-wide to instill new values of diversity and inclusion. Chris Taylor, the museum's chief inclusion officer, has devised a process to embed inclusive practices that are values-based.

Creating a shared vocabulary is one of the key steps. A goal is to refocus all staff on the urgency of inclusion and to build a pipeline for a more diverse workforce. This approach is having an impact as a model for other museums.[25]

The theme of change runs through most contemporary leadership thinking. As we consider the Kotter approach there are similarities to the lessons of Jim Collins's writings that were outlined in chapter 2. Collins talks about getting the right people on the bus (alignment and guiding coalition), the importance of Big Hairy Audacious Goals (vision), and persistent will of the leader (communications and consolidating gains). Another management publication that has gained credibility is Chip and Dan Heath's *Switch*, written in 2011.[26] This book is filled with case studies that highlight change. The Heaths advocate for finding the "bright spots" or small examples within the organization that represent success. What works well already and does not need to change, for example. The book is less concerned with radical change and more on the practical implementation of change. How will it work operationally? We need to invest in it. Not only do we need engaging visions, but also we need to describe the outcome that will make an *emotional* connection. Like Kotter, *Switch* suggests that the organization should move forward with small wins or "bite-sized steps." An important factor is assigning staff to serve as coaches or internal change leaders. An emphasis on building on strengths (the "bright spots") is a practical and positive approach to change. At the same time, they see value in asking questions about lessons learned from failure. Using internal change agents has been a very successful approach as these individuals can work to persuade fellow staff members of the value of the vision.

As we consider change in the organization we need to address the reality of contemporary external demands as described in the beginning of this chapter. In a world challenged by reactions to immigration, poverty, racial biases, and freedom of speech, museums are feeling the pressure to provide a safe haven or to set an example for the important values of our society. Museums need to take risks to speak out in support of their values in public programming, exhibitions, and collecting.

In response to the need for inclusion, the shifts in economic power, the huge transformations of technological innovation, the shift to a sharing economy, the challenge of maintaining resilience and relevance, the growing fragmentation of individual values, community concerns, and our ability to process vast amounts of data, we need to accept that turbulence and disruption are a way of life. In fact organizational change is now a fundamental expectation for today's leaders. Meeting the challenge of disruptive change was the topic of Clayton Christensen and Michael Overdorf's 2000 *Harvard Business Review* article.[27] Certainly today's world is even more complex. Their article described the reality of start-up companies that challenge and sometimes conquer traditional ones. The example of traditional higher education curriculum being out of date in face of for-profit online learning services, the reality of the sharing economy transforming commerce (same day delivery), and the rise of robotics and artificial intelligence as a threat to the labor force are examples. Can museums meet the challenges of inclusivity, accessibility, and a myriad of alternative modes of education and entertainment that the public now demands? The constant invention of new and better data management and information sharing leaves us in the dust. Museum Hack now may be providing a more entertaining museum learning experience than the traditional docent. Museums need to be flexible and forward thinking. As improvements in providing services escalate traditional organizations will need to turn their resources toward improving products. Resistance to these efforts will hamper progress. Incubator models now make sense and museums need to follow suit. Christiansen and Overdorf advocated that corporations seek to establish internal teams to design new products, working independently of the existing organizational structure. In some cases the corporation could create a spin-off to develop products or to acquire or merge with another firm that provides talented staff and technology solutions. Museums rarely do this. An example might be those larger museums that establish for-profit business ventures entities for product development.

Not only corporations but foundations too are undergoing change. For example under the leadership of Darren Walker the Ford Foundation has adopted a new philosophy and funding priority to combat inequality. The Foundation has a sense of urgency to redesign their funding goals to reduce programs from thirty-five to fifteen, to establish interdisciplinary teams, and to put in place more accountability in building realistic budgets and cost analysis.[28]

The Leader's Role in Change

Stewardship of the change process takes a skilled leader. It demands a balance of power in the organization and at the same time a tolerance for ambiguity. Change is messy and all the answers are not apparent. Sharing power, assuring accountability in decision making, empathy, and a reliance on a learning organization are critical. In the next chapter we will explore modern leadership qualities. Not only does there need to be commitment but also the ability to set priorities and practice sound decision systems. An example of a wide-scale culture change in the for-profit world is that of Microsoft Corporation. Under the leadership of CEO Satya Nadella and Chief Human Resources Officer Kathleen Hogan their overly complacent workforce culture was overhauled. An emphasis on innovation, new ideas, embracing diversity, a new vocabulary for operations, and cross-functional collaboration are components of this culture change program. An organization in the Aristocracy phase of their life cycle, the need for cultural revitalization was clear.[29]

Understanding the life cycle of the museum is critical. Change will occur best at the level of Prime. In the following chapter we will examine the best practices of leadership in the for-profit and nonprofit arena and how these play out in the museum. In summary, change can be a positive for individuals and for organizations if the leadership is effective, sensitive, courageous, and persistent. Even in a time of crisis there can be positive results. This book will examine how change is managed in museums and those creative leaders who serve as positive role models. In particular the case studies detailed in chapter 8 are excellent examples of change leadership.

Discussion Questions

1. What stage is your museum on the organizational life cycle? Given that how do you approach an important change process?
2. How would you approach the need for reorganizing the museum given a sudden downturn in the economy? What structural changes make the most sense for the short term or for longer term?
3. How do Kotter's eight stages work in a small museum? What would be an appropriate use of this philosophy in your museum?
4. What steps should a museum take to assure a smooth transition for staff that are affected by change?

Notes

1. Lily Allen, "Getty Trust Announces Major Downsizing," *Art in America*, May 1, 2012, http://www.artinamericamagazine.com/news-features/news/getty-lay-offs.

2. Peggy McGlone, "Hirshhorn Ends Docent Program, Telling Volunteers That They Are No Longer Needed," *Washington Post*, October 30, 2014, https://www.washingtonpost.com/entertainment/museums/hirshhorn-ends-docent-program-telling-volunteers-that-they-are-no-longer-needed/2014/10/30/24d1b8aa-5ec6-11e4-8b9e-2ccdac31a031_story.html?utm_term=.55dbaaec10ea.

3. Adrienne Berard, "Colonia Williamsburg Quietly Lays Off Dozens of Employees in Reorganization Effort," *WY Daily*, January 12, 2017, http://wydaily.com/2017/01/12/colonial-williamsburg-quietly-lays-off-dozens-of-employees-in-reorganization-effort/?platform=hootsuite.

4. Peggy McGlone, "Newseum Lays Off 26 Employees about 10 percent of Staff as Financial Struggles Continue," *Washington Post*, January 24, 2017, https://www.washingtonpost.com/news/arts-and-entertainment/wp/2017/01/24/newseum-lays-off-26-employees-about-10-percent-of-staff-as-financial-struggles-continue/?utm_term=.0ccb1c9a093a.

5. Steve Roberts Jr., "Colonial Williamsburg to Outsource Operations, Announces Layoffs," *WY Daily*, June 29, 2017, http://wydaily.com/2017/06/29/colonial-williamsburg-fundamentally-restructures-citing-dire-financials-business-news/.

6. Martha Morris et al., "Benchmarking Studies, 1995–2000," unpublished internal reports of surveys of thirty U.S. museums by the National Museum of American History, Smithsonian Institution.

7. Heritage Preservation, "Heritage Health Index," 2004 report, http://www.conservation-us.org/our-organizations/foundation-(faic)/initiatives/heritage-preservation.

8. The Metropolitan Museum of Art, "About the Costume Institute," http://www.metmuseum.org/about-the-met/curatorial-departments/the-costume-institute.

9. Julia Halperin, "As a Generation of Directors Reaches Retirement, Fresh Faces Prepare to Take over US Museums," *Art Newspaper*, June 2, 2015, http://theartnewspaper.com/news/museums/fresh-faces-set-to-take-over-at-the-top-/.

10. Smithsonian Institution Strategic Plan 2017–2022, https://www.si.edu/strategicplan.

11. Michael M Kaiser, *The Art of the Turnaround, Creating and Maintaining Healthy Arts Organizations* (Waltham, MA: Brandeis University Press 2008), 1–14.

12. The life cycle of organizations is outlined by Ichak Adizes, *Managing Corporate Life Cycles* (Paramus, NJ: Prentice Hall, 1999).

13. Robin Pogrebin, "Metropolitan Museum's Director Resigns under Pressure," *New York Times,* February 28, 2017, https://www.nytimes.com/2017/02/28/arts/design/met-museum-director-resigns-thomas-campbell.html?_r=0.

14. Elaine Gurian, "Moving the Museum," in *Institutional Trauma* (Washington, DC: American Association of Museums, 1995), 34–51.

15. Judith Dobrzynski, "Boston Museum's Restructuring Sows Fear among U.S. Curators," *New York Times*, July 8, 1999. B1.

16. Paul Strebel, "Why Do Employees Resist Change," *Harvard Business Review* (May/June 1996): 86–92.

17. William Bridges, *Managing Transitions* (New York: Addison-Wesley, 1991).

18. Author was deputy director of the museum and with Director Spencer Crew designed the planning and reorganization effort.

19. "Merger Case Study: Cincinnati Museum Center at Union Terminal," Strategic Restructuring: Partnership Options for Nonprofits. La Piana Consulting, http://www.La Piana.org/resources/cases/mergers/09_2003.html.

20. John P. Kotter, *Leading Change* (Boston: Harvard Business School Press, 1996).

21. Robert R. Janes, "Embracing Organizational Change, A Work in Progress," in *Museum Management and Marketing*, ed. R. Sandell and R. Janes (New York: Routledge, 2007), 67–81.

22. This description is from firsthand knowledge of the author who was a member of senior management that designed and led the change process from 1993 to 2001.

23. Brian Ferriso interview, National Arts Strategies, 2013, http://www.artstrategies.org/leadership_tools/videos/2013/03/20/how-do-you-re-engineer-a-cultural-institution-with-a-long-history-and-numerous-stakeholders/#.WTMyvRiZPox.

24. Amy Gilman, "Institutionalizing Innovation at the Toledo Museum of Art," in *Fundraising and Strategic Planning: Innovative Approaches for Museums*, ed. Juilee Decker (Lanham, MD: Rowman and Littlefield, 2015), 103–110.

25. Chris Taylor lecture to GW MSTD University Seminar on March 9, 2017.

26. Chip Heath and Dan Heath, *Switch: How to Change Things When Change Is Hard* (Waterville, ME: Thorndike Press, 2011).

27. Clayton Christensen and Michael Overdorf, "Meeting the Challenge of Disruptive Change," *Harvard Business Review* 78, no. 2 (2000): 67–76.

28. Darren Walker, "Moving the Ford Foundation Forward," November 9, 2015, http://us10.campaign-archive1.com/?u=3f89269c6132144b6f1c5ce78&id=4fe9d631dc.

29. Jack Robinson, "Culture Change Agents," Human Resource Executive Online, September 19, 2016, http://www.hreonline.com/HRE/view/story.jhtml?id=534361119.

CONTEMPORARY LEADERSHIP MODELS

In considering the challenge of turbulence and change outlined in the previous chapter, the role of leadership has become central to organizational success. This chapter will discuss the qualifications needed for today's leaders. Specifically this chapter will examine several individual styles including Level 5, systems leadership, servant leadership, and adaptive leadership. Models of effective approaches and the importance of values and organizational culture will be discussed. The fundamental issue of collaborative models versus more traditional approaches of the individual at the top will be introduced. Building on the lessons of chapter 3 it is important to look at leaders who are crafting successful change programs, through an emphasis on values.

Organizational Leadership Styles

Defining leadership is a moving target. Many views exist and all are valid. Peter Drucker, often anointed as the father of modern business theory, has described leaders as those who are willing to listen, to make themselves understood, and then realize that "the task matters, you are the servant."[1] Drucker sees the effective executive as one that exercises compassion, teaching, and learning to "make it easy for people to do their work, easy to have results, and easy to enjoy their work."[2]

Modern literature on leadership also acknowledges the importance of followership. You can promote inspiring ideas, but without followers, nothing will happen. As was discussed in chapter 3, the social contract between leaders and their staff is one critical factor in leading change. Followers vary in their reactions to leaders. Followers may be isolated, indifferent, resistant, or passionate cheerleaders. In reality individuals in the organization may be both leaders and followers. Middle managers play both roles. The factor of loyalty is always at play. The effective follower needs self-management, independence, a positive attitude, and opportunities to excel. In working with followers sometimes a leader chooses to work with individuals who are their assumed rivals or potential opponents. This allows the leader to consciously build a positive relationship and to be aware of dissention. Speaking truth to power is a strategy that allows followers to provide solutions to difficult problems. Strong leaders understand this.[3]

Understanding the impact and meaning of leadership in the modern organization is the subject of constant debate. Today we look at leadership from many angles including political, social, economic, and cultural. Leaders have tremendous impact on the success or failure of all sectors of our society. They are at their best when they influence the work of others toward positive end goals. The difference between leadership and management has been debated for many years and the distinction needs to be explored. Although leadership is what we all are looking for to guide our organizations through turbulent times, competent managers are needed as well.[4]

Clearly there is a distinction between leaders and managers (see textbox 4.1). We know however that these traits can be blended in individuals. Depending on the situation that faces the organization, a visionary leader may also need to plan, supervise, and evaluate individuals in the workplace. Managers can also step out of their administrative role to take risks, and dream big about the changes needed in the organization. We will look at factors that compel organizations to seek these types of individuals.

Considering the organizational success characteristics that were discussed in chapter 2, we know that Jim Collins advocated for the humility and focus of a Level 5 leader. This leader is both modest and

Textbox 4.1.
MANAGERS VERSUS LEADERS

Managers Do Things Right	Leaders Do the Right Thing
• Organize work	• Create vision
• Develop plans	• Encourage risk taking
• Hire and train staff	• See the big picture
• Evaluate programs and staff	• Develop basic values
• Acquire resources	• Empower and stretch staff
• Analyze needs/results	• Listen, facilitate, and coach

selfless, preferring to give credit to the staff rather than bask in personal accolades. They also exert the will to produce superior results setting exacting standards.[5] Daniel Goleman of Harvard University defined enduring characteristics of effective leadership in his writings on Emotional Intelligence. In the corporate setting he found that success was equated with personalities who demonstrated self-awareness, self-regulation, motivation, empathy, and social skills. All of these traits are further defined by trustworthiness, openness to change, optimism, commitment, cross-cultural sensitivity, and teambuilding.[6] Rather than intellectual prowess, the successful leader needs to exhibit personal traits that are focused on group behavior and individual awareness. Like Collins, Goleman understands the importance of focus in leadership. He speaks of empathy in understanding other perspectives, and responsiveness to the needs of others. Understanding the wider world, being a good listener, and being tuned in to the views of those working in the organization will lead to more innovation.

Another dimension of leadership research is the work of Peter Senge who advocates for organizations that place emphasis on individual learning and understanding. He describes a holistic approach that includes

• Systems thinking: understanding the big picture
• Personal mastery: self-knowledge
• Mental models: recognizing and overcoming biases in thinking
• Shared vision: creating a vision that all employees can buy into
• Team learning: a culture of analyzing lessons learned

Senge's theories were developed in the early 1990s and as a result his influence is evident today where we see a more collaborative approach to leadership, seeking to build a shared vision. Systems thinking—seeing the big picture—is not meant only for the CEOs, but should be an attribute of leaders at all levels. Successful leaders both enlist all staff in managing the organization and promote the ability to learn from experiences. The reference to mental models is of value in overcoming misunderstandings based on ingrained assumptions about the attitudes of colleagues in the workplace. Senge's most lasting theory is the emphasis on team learning, where reflection on program goals and work process can lead to improvements. For example, in the museum field a process of team evaluation of successes and failures in projects leads to improvements for the future.[7]

Servant Leadership

The term *servant leadership* was first defined in the landmark work of Robert Greenleaf an employee of telecommunication giant AT&T in the 1970s. He believed that leadership is not based on wielding power, but in providing support. Leaders provide resources, train, mentor, and reward. Decision making is shared. This servant approach has been growing in popularity for the past thirty years and we see it reflected in the writings of Drucker, as well as Collins and Goleman. The servant leader ideas are about releasing control and abandoning top down decisions. These leaders help employees. They help people face reality and mobilize change efforts, seek opportunities for the future, listen and display empathy, and seek out and encourage the development of grassroots leaders. A servant leader still needs to set goals and to recognize the good work of employees, but in all ways, their role is to enable individuals to succeed.

The opposite of the servant leader is the *narcissist*. Much has been written about this personality trait and how it plays out in the workplace, and society at large. In sum, these leaders are cited for incredible breakthroughs and creativity, delivered with charm and force. Narcissists are excellent communicators, can create compelling visions, and inspire followers. However, there are productive and nonproductive narcissists. For example, Steve Jobs was described as abrasive, dominating, and arrogant. No one would argue that he was transformational and in the end, productive. But the downside of narcissism is that these leaders are self-centered, do not trust others, and dominate decision making. Collaboration is not in their vocabulary. Motivated by power and a desire to be admired, we can only imagine how this type of leader could ruin the morale and aspirations of the workforce.[8]

In reflecting on servant and narcissistic styles we see swings between the yin and yang of leadership. In some instances the strong and charismatic leader is most admired. At other times the humble and participative style is preferred. In fact leadership style may be more related to the life cycle of the organization or the situation at hand. Flexibility is critical. Studies have shown that humble and collaborative styles inspire workers. Despite this a "romance of leadership" attracts us to the charismatic personality and their vision for change. In times of crisis in fact we may tend to favor this type of leader who will solve all of our problems.[9] In the modern world of rapid technological change, various start-ups tend to attract this type of individual leader. Critical articles about both Amazon and Uber have revealed a workplace mentality that is far from empathetic. Reports of workers pitted against each other in regard to project outcomes along with long hours and secrecy about new innovations reveal an atmosphere of stress and tension. Jeff Bezos, the CEO of Amazon, has noted that "conflict brings about innovation." The organization is focused on constant innovation and customer needs. Peer review and competition is expected. Metrics drive decisions and individual reviews. This atmosphere has led to multiple complaints and sets up a dilemma for anyone seeking work-life balance.[10] A toxic workplace was also seen in start-up company Uber, with allegations of sexual harassment and a culture of disrespect for workers. Fortunately, there is a growing realization that workplace culture has an impact on the brand satisfaction of consumers. These situations are easily exposed by social and mainstream media and thus the human resource function of the organization becomes more important.[11] In reflecting on the workplace atmosphere and leadership style we need to consider the context. Leaders may actually need to employ varying styles depending on the situation at hand. The more flexible the leader in employing a style the better. Daniel Goleman has reflected on this issue in assuring us that an authoritative style may be best in a crisis, while a democratic style is important to build buy in and inclusion, and a coaching style will work well in building employee strengths.[12]

Adaptive Leadership

Perhaps the most relevant theory of twenty-first-century leadership is the work of Ronald Heifetz. Adaptive leadership is necessary in a time of constant and disruptive change. Espousing a process that engages the entire organization, effort goes into understanding how a group can make smart decisions. Groups throughout the organization can be responsive to the imperative of constant change. The adaptive leader encourages conversations about what is essential, and inspires curiosity and empathy; and with a focus on reality, data, and facts, often creates an atmosphere of productive discomfort. Similar to the theories of Action Learning, the adaptive process often involves a small group of diverse individuals (skills, responsibilities, backgrounds) that tackle a problem. Through reflective inquiry the leader poses questions that result in better understanding among the group members. Opinions are not as important as facts.[13] A focus on positive and open-minded solutions to problems is fundamental. As we look at the topic of innovation in chapter 6, this approach will be examined again.

The writings of Chip and Dan Heath also reflect a similar approach. In their book *Decisive*, they advocate for seeking external views on a problem, allowing time and distance for reflection and avoiding emotions.[14] Posing questions such as "what will our future leadership or workforce think about this decision" and "what other options do we have" allow for a careful process. In the museum we might be looking at any number of issues such as rebranding, using social networking for fundraising, or seeking a faster, smarter, and cheaper way to create changing exhibitions. All of these activities are driven by a commitment to internal communications.

Leadership Is a Conversation

Jim Collins talks about the diffuse power structure of the nonprofit entity. Effectiveness in leadership means being a great communicator with all constituencies and all levels of the organization. The importance of the leader becoming a servant of the follower is underscored in other ways. Corporate models have evolved around the area of internal communications where the function of "conversation" now provides a model. This approach values intimacy, dialogue, personal transparency, and listening. Leaders are expected to reach out to employees at all levels, engaging in dialogue around strategic goals. This philosophy advocates for "open book" information sharing, trust, and even 360-degree evaluation. This can be via face-to-face meetings or telepresence. Examples in industry include the long-term CEO of Cisco Systems, John Chambers, who holds employee forums without the presence of senior managers. He also publishes a monthly video blog shared throughout the organization. Conversation is meant to stimulate committed employees who are encouraged to speak publically about their work, and to share innovative ideas as internal thought leaders.[15]

The transformational leader has been touted as our twenty-first-century savior. This individual is risk taking, determined, adaptive, focused, values-driven, and emotionally intelligent. Do we have examples? *Harvard Business Review* regularly features the most admired leaders in the corporate sector. Surveys completed in 2015 featured the CEO of Novo Nordisk, a Swedish pharmaceutical company with a mission for social responsibility. We have seen that this value is now a fundamental expectation for many successful corporations. The CEO Lars Sorensen described himself as consensus-oriented in building a leadership team, as opposed to being the lionized individual achiever at the top. He also believes that the pay gap between the senior management and staff should be small in order to build trust and morale among the workforce. Sorensen emphasizes the importance of communications and innovations with long-term impact.[16] These traits reflect the prevailing preference for the Servant and Level 5 leader. But research published in 2017 has revealed that the behavior of great CEOs is more complex. A data analysis of 17,000 senior executives was completed over a ten-year study based on executive performance assessments.[17] Four behaviors were characteristic of the high-performing CEO:

- Decision making with speed and conviction
- Understanding stakeholder needs through disciplined communication
- Proactive adaptability with focus on the long term
- Reliability in producing results

These characteristics are more in line with that of Goleman in regard to focus, Heifetz in regard to adaptability, and Collins in regard to discipline. No matter how we slice it, the profile of a modern leader is multifaceted. Charisma is not even mentioned in these studies.

Successful Museum Models

Unfortunately we see a lot of museums working under an outdated model. Robert Janes has written about the downside of a system that favors the lone director. This individual is expected to operate with authority, to serve as the sole decision maker, and a focal point for the organization. The hierarchical leader is often overburdened and either out of touch with the external world or too concerned about a safe approach. Today we see directors paid exorbitant salaries while museum staff fight for a living wage. These highly paid CEOs have "power, authority, and privilege" where shared authority is absent. In today's museum as we see in the corporate models a group leadership model should be more effective. Flat organizational structures, team-based decisions, and shared authority all have a better success record.[18]

In addition to the issues of power, museum leaders today need to exercise both their management skills and leadership talent. The responsibilities of running nonprofits and museums demand financial acumen, fundraising success, emotional intelligence, courage, enthusiasm, teambuilding, vision, stakeholder outreach, and willingness to delegate. The importance of communications as described above cannot be overlooked. An example of the fundamental value of communications was highlighted in the work of Paul Redmond at Longwood Gardens. In rolling out a new strategic plan, the staff were at the center of the dialogue in town hall meetings or in small focus groups where issues of "vocabulary" and values were hashed out. And as anxiety rose in regard to the implementation of the plan, the staff engaged in "stop/start" discussions that clarified priorities.[19]

One factor that has been emphasized in discussing leadership in museums is the need to embrace mission. And in this regard one often hears the word "passion" in describing the nonprofit leader. Sherene Suchy researched the topic in her seminal 1994 publication *Leading with Passion*. Her research involved interviews with over forty-five directors and assistant directors of art museums. Passion was attached to collections, social impact, education, and discovery, to entrepreneurial efforts and to constructive discontent. These traits continue to resonate.[20] When we consider this trait, the relationship between passion and vision and the adaptive and decisive traits noted above would apply to museum leaders who are breaking ground with new initiatives including building projects. Consider the work of Lonnie Bunch at the National Museum of African American History and Culture or Alice Greenwald at the 9/11 Memorial Museum. They along with others have persevered to create impressive museums making a significant contribution to issues of social justice.

Complementing the passion of leaders is a more "mindful" approach. This emphasis allows for more focus on priority work. Museums can be plagued by skeptical and negative staff who are stressed by the changing external environment and the ambiguity and complexity of the modern world. Thus staff have to be given power to help solve the inevitable problems and be part of a culture of strategic thinking. Here there is a continuing emphasis on examination of strengths, weaknesses, opportunities, and threats (SWOT analysis) and scenario planning. In an ideal world the leader manages holistically and staff are engaged in understanding the big picture, and seeking strategies to adapt to a changing world. Values-based decision making includes focus on diversity, inclusion, social justice, respect, and empathy. Not only will the leader be in touch with community but also focused on the triple bottom line of social responsibility, environmental stewardship, and economic strength. In a public role the leader is also required to serve as advocate for both the organization and the social impact they are making. When we discuss the issue of core values we are talking about those which impact both decision making and individual behaviors. Most organizations have a set of values sometimes written, sometimes unstated, but they are fundamental guidelines.

The research of Anne Ackerson and Joan Baldwin cataloged personal traits of today's museum leaders. These individuals were characterized by their intentionality, self-awareness, agility, and communications skills. These leaders believe in shared decision making, connecting to the community, multiple approaches to serving the mission, and intense listening skills. The leaders they studied believe in nurturing relationships, taking risks, and seeking feedback from all stakeholders. These individuals can zoom in or zoom out on a variety of problems, balancing practical and visionary solutions. For example, Burt Logan, CEO of the Ohio Historical Society, was profiled. He wisely noted that a mature leader needs to frame the questions, not know all the answers. In addition, he believes in a leadership team where everyone can be a leader. Finally, he recounts the importance of leading change, listening, learning, and being nimble while embracing values.[21]

Janes, Suchy, and Ackerson and Baldwin all are converging on a modern leadership paradigm. Their thinking describes the profile of museum leaders in their research and also provides a counterbalance to the well-known dysfunctions of the nonprofit sector. Examining these issues reveals many nonprofits lack sound leadership in the form of strategic plans or succession plans. Studies also reveal that middle managers are unsure about the strategic direction of their nonprofit. And not surprisingly staff members are not being given professional development opportunities. This can lead to high levels of turnover. Furthermore, insufficient funding is applied to the areas of marketing and communications; both needed to assure public support of the mission.[22] Some of these same issues were evident in the 2017 AAM/BoardSource report discussed in chapter 2. There are many reasons that nonprofits are not successful. Leadership is a challenge and many obstacles stand in the way of success. Two areas need to be examined to understand these challenges. One is the reality of turnover, the other the social attitudes about gender and diversity. The issue of turnover is related to two factors: the retirement of older generations and the stress of the job. The latter has been the subject of numerous studies including CompassPoint's landmark study of nonprofit leadership, *Daring to Lead*. Over 3,000 individuals were surveyed in this 2011 study. The following are highlights.[23]

- 65 percent of leadership plan to leave within five years
- Only 17 percent have a succession plan
- Performance reviews are not done
- Financial solvency is poor
- Dissatisfaction with human resource management
- Lack of leadership development
- Board dysfunction

The majority of nonprofit leaders in this study were women, who complained about receiving lower pay than male counterparts. Despite that, the women claim to be motivated by the mission not the salary. Highest stress was found in smaller organization with budgets of $500,000 to $1,000,000.

Women Leaders: The Dilemma

The above findings reflect the museum field as well. As reported by the Mellon Foundation in 2015, and again in 2017 women in the art museum workforce reportedly make less than men in comparable positions.[24] And yet the research of Goleman in 2016 leads to the conclusion that women are better leaders due to their emotional intelligence.[25] Despite this there are reasons why this is happening. Social norms play an important part. Sheryl Sandberg's landmark publication *Lean In* chronicled many stories of women failing to be recognized as leaders in the corporate workforce. Some of the reasoning is that women are not leaning in or bold enough to rise to the top. She notes the "Tiara effect" as an example of women who work hard and think that they will automatically be recognized for their contributions. She also speaks about the inability of women to sit at the table in meetings, customarily taking a seat in the back of the room.[26]

How women rise to the top of organizations is of constant speculation and interest. If Goleman has found that women exhibit emotional intelligence are they also closer to the transformational model needed to succeed in the twenty-first century? Two examples can explain some of the nuances. In 2012 a fascinating case study occurred at the University of Virginia where the president and board chair (both women) clashed in a fundamental issue of leadership style. The issue involved the Board Chair Helen Dragas's desire to oust the president, Theresa Sullivan, for her lack of vision. Sullivan as the university's first female president with a long history of higher education leadership was moving in a consensus driven and incremental manner to implement changes at the university. The board chair with corporate experience felt that the pace was too slow and not visionary. She determined to more or less unilaterally fire Sullivan. Push back from the staff and faculty was immediate. Some board members were not in line with the decision. The event became a national story. The faculty was threatened by a dominant board chair that appeared to be out of touch with the values of the university. The decision to fire Sullivan was reversed and she continued to run the university until announcing her resignation in 2017.[27] Was this due to innate biases about women leaders?

Other examples have illustrated the value of women leading large nonprofit organizations. In 2014 the Kennedy Center for Performing Arts named a new president, Deborah Rutter.[28] Rutter replaced a long-term visionary and strongly focused leader, Michael Kaiser, who had raised hundreds of millions of dollars, created new themed programs, and planned a major expansion while launching a consulting program to save arts organizations around the world. Rutter had a long history of running symphonies in several cities and came to her new post with a reputation as an effective team builder. She has deep experience in the classical music world but also earned her MBA. She is known for emphasizing collaboration, innovation, and community engagement. In a 2015 interview she noted that "I am involved but not a microman-ager. There is no chance that I could be. I am deeply involved but fully delegate to people who have the responsibility." Rutter believes her job is about motivation and leadership. "I am not a coercer or a dictator but if I feel strongly about something I will advocate for it."[29] After three years on the job, Rutter sparked some controversy for her efforts to popularize programming, for creating a new strategic plan, and for implementing "business practices."

Organizational change is difficult and moving swiftly to implement new programs can create waves.[30] A critical factor for CEOs is their ability to build strong relationships with their board chair. This is one of the most telling factors in leadership success as noted in the 2016 survey by BoardSource and AAM. It is among several reasons why we see turnover at the top including demanding boards, poor fundraising success, overly ambitious programs, and burnout as noted in *Daring to Lead*, mentioned above.

Examples of women leaders in museums are numerous. Two are worth highlighting for the ability to turnaround failing organizations. Della Watkins became director of the Taubman Museum in Roanoke, Virginia in 2013. She was formally a museum educator at the Virginia Museum of Fine Arts. The Taubman opened to the public in a new starchitect-designed museum in 2008. For many years the museum struggled to draw audiences and raise sufficient funds to become sustainable. Their story has been chronicled by researchers at the University of Chicago and University of Pennsylvania. The bottom line was that board members were forced to bail out the museum for several years as well as cut staff and operations. Watkins came to the museum with excellent experience in public programming and a positive attitude. Her first challenge was to focus on the financials and move slowly with incremental changes. Over the years efforts to rebuild endowment and stage traveling exhibitions have made a difference. The museum is out of the woods and has been accredited by the AAM.[31]

What is needed to rescue a museum? The Southern Oregon Historical Society is a case of a museum that was close to going out of business. In 2009 Allison Weiss took over as executive director. The museum had lost significant county funding in the recession and was forced to suspend operations while they planned for a revival. A focus on the community was the saving factor. Weiss wrote her story for an article in *History News*. Several actions saved the organization including deaccessioning, leasing properties, outreach to community history groups, and a children's museum, a new board, and volunteer support.[32]

Looking at the experiences of Weiss and Watkins we see that the resilient leader is focused on moving quickly from dissecting the current situation to looking forward. They ask pointed questions that will help overcome the knee jerk negative thinking that holds the organization back. Leaders need to ask what features can be improved? What impact can they have personally on the situation? How can the negative factors be contained? What can be done right now to move us forward?

Looking Forward

In reflecting the leadership theory and trends of the twenty-first century, we see the lone director model is rapidly becoming obsolete. The successful organization has a culture of collaboration. Everyone in the organization needs to be a part of the problem-solving team. Business literature has studied the response to recessions for example. These studies show that successful comebacks are made by companies that cut costs not only to improve efficiency, but spend more on marketing and R&D while staying close to understanding the customer's needs as they re-invent their businesses. And, they practice a disciplined approach to gathering data and making sound decisions. Museum leaders who provide open book management practices are more likely going to be successful. An excellent example is that of Ellen Rosenthal, former CEO of Conner Prairie Museum in Indiana. As she shared at the AAM annual meeting in Minneapolis in 2012, her staff participated in a sophisticated financial literacy program that taught them to read and create budgets and financial reports plus the basics of feasibility planning and decision making. Giving staff the opportunity to create what if scenarios for cutting programs or assessing viability of new ideas is groundbreaking. It takes the mystery out of what senior management is doing.[33] Decision systems need to carefully consider mission, resources, risks, costs, and legal and ethical concerns. And any high stakes decision needs to be made in a participative manner assuring input from affected staff. Once decisions are made the implementation process needs to be clear including the roles and responsibilities of staff. For example an approach to decision making at the San Diego Museum of Man under the leadership of Micah Parzen employs a matrix to test new ideas. A checklist allows the museum staff to score new ideas on a rank between 1 and 5 on twelve different factors. This is then used as a discussion document on strategic programs. Both data fluency and rapid prototyping are expected responsibilities of museum leaders in the future.[34]

Looking forward we know that museum leaders need to be much more flexible and open to change. They must share ideas with colleagues and seek best practices from many quarters. They need to be experts at financial planning and fundraising, able to take risks, alert to building community partnerships, comfortable with ambiguity, and accessible. Leaders need to provide learning opportunities for their staff and value the internal culture of the museum. And there is value in adopting the principles of servant leadership that were espoused by Robert Greenleaf. Every leader exists to nurture staff who in turn serve the public.

Leadership Transition and the Interim Leader

As mentioned in chapter 3 the Metropolitan Museum of Art has gone through a painful leadership transition. As it faced growing pains with a new director and consequent deficit spending, the museum needed to make a transition to a new structure. The board determined to restructure top leadership to create a senior CEO position over the museum director. As this transition took place, questions and concerns were raised about the museum's culture and the role of a director with deep programmatic experience but little business skill.[35]

Change at the top is one of the most important challenges that organizations face. Sometimes the transition is smooth where a trusted staff member has been groomed to take over when the director retires. Other times it's a dramatic change. A leader is fired or suddenly resigns. A museum goes through a merger. Or as is common in our field, a better job lures your director away. How do we assure a successful transition when there is no obvious new director on the horizon?

I became interested in this issue as an interim leader in the mid-1990s. Both the director and deputy director were in acting posts for one year at the National Museum of American History. There is much ambiguity and complexity with interims. There are limits due to uncertainty as to who will be in charge eventually. How much power can you really exercise? How much can you change? It's difficult if the acting person is a *former peer*. Both the acting director and I had been peers and even had worked for other members of the staff in our careers.

When a leader goes it creates different reactions in the staff:

- Some feel betrayed or abandoned
- Others feels guilty because they are pleased
- There can be a lot of rumors, a lot of jockeying for position

The ensuing chaos needs to be corralled through the swift implementation of an interim plan.

Often an interim leader will be one of the members of the board or a trusted senior staff member. Another option would be hiring a consultant to serve as interim director. The selection process is one that should be subject to board policies and procedures, but often that is not the case. The critical factor is the need to specify what the interim leader needs to do. Will they serve as a caretaker pending hiring the permanent director? Are they needed to serve as a turnaround specialist in a time of chaos? A fundamental question then is how much power do these individuals have to make changes. In most cases an interim will be in place for six to nine months during an executive search period.

Therefore, it is not likely that dramatic changes would be possible in this time frame. The individual has the option to be a caretaker or to focus on areas of clear need such as balancing the budget. A lame duck leader has little clout and perhaps the board has a tight rein on their actions. Authority may be limited. This creates a weak leader who may find making any change is a challenge. And the individual in the interim role may be less inclined to make any decision that will impact the long term. In a more forward-thinking role this individual can work to create a transition plan in anticipating the incoming leader. At the Museum of American History, acting director Spencer Crew and I worked on a strategic plan with the museum staff. This included engaging all staff in planning, bringing in experts from outside the museum, and providing for a lot of input to a strategic assessment.

Studies of the role of the acting director in museums reveal a number of findings. A national study of 210 museums in 2000 reported some troubling findings. Fundraising success dropped due to the lack of a permanent director, some staff left the museum during the interim period, and the level of anxiety about decisions at the top was noticeable.[36]

Robert Goler's survey conducted in the 1990s found a widespread use of outside consultants in the role of interim. The advantage of these individuals was that they were a fresh set of eyes with an ability to recommend changes that would sustain the organization or rectify problems. At the same time when an existing staff member was temporarily promoted to "acting" director there were some negative and positive results. The relationship with former peers was sometimes a challenge and if the interim leader was not selected for the job, a distinct number of these individuals left the museum. On the positive side these individuals did gain new skills and perspectives that assisted in their long-term career development. And some were promoted to new positions after the permanent director was hired.[37]

Succession Planning

Given the fact that museum boards have a poor track record in developing succession plans as reported in the 2017 BoardSource report mentioned in chapter 2, the reality is that the transition process will likely be messy. An executive search process is costly and time-consuming. Staff tend to be anxious and are guaranteed to be circulating rumors throughout the process. Looking at recent literature on the topic of corporate succession there are several best practices to consider.[38] First, create opportunities for existing staff to get cross-functional experience, such as leading a new project, which gives the board a chance to test the skills of rising stars. Second, a savvy board will know the bench depth of staff in the organization, looking carefully at the senior management team and understanding their strengths and weaknesses. Third, be sure to create performance metrics that can be applied to the current CEO and senior staff and evaluate them regularly. Fourth, maintain a list of potential outside candidates. This entails an informal assessment of strong leaders at other organizations who could be considered in the case of a leadership vacuum. Increasing emphasis on soft skills was found to be a fundamental step in the CEO search. Many boards will assign a few key members to lead the search. These individuals need to know the critical challenges facing the organization before launching a formal search. Throughout the process the board needs to keep an open mind about the candidates and realize no one is perfect. After a selection is made a careful process of onboarding will assure a better transition. Understanding the capabilities and concerns of all staff in the organization is imperative. Not just the goals and the financials, but the human side of their new staff. First actions speak loudly. CEOs should be willing to make important decisions early. In addition include a rigorous effort to get out of the office and meet everyone, see the entire facility, meet every guard, and docent, and spend time with the visitors. Ask questions and be respectful. The practice of overlap between the old and new director should be considered. An outgoing director will have much to share with the incumbent. At the same time too much overlap can confuse staff and board. Examples of hiring goals might include the Hirshhorn Museum's recruitment of Melissa Chui to attract new and younger audience, rebuild the board, and bring in exciting international talent.[39]

The Director's Life Cycle

Is there a step-by-step approach to building one's career as a chief executive? How do you assure success? Charles F. Bryan Jr. chronicled his story in a revealing article in *Museum News* in 2007. As president and CEO of the Virginia Historical Society for nearly twenty years, he experienced three stages of growth as a leader. He spoke of the early years of learning and gradual change. The next phase included significant shaping building strong relationships with the board and staff while implementing a strategic plan. In the third stage (after ten years) the CEO needs to consider sustaining success, work/life balance, and planning an exit strategy.[40] This is the story of a highly successful individual. But as we know everyone has a different story and many factors can impact success. In considering the growth and tenure of a museum director, we will look more closely at this in chapter 8 on case studies, including the current director of the Virginia Historical Society. Every individual will have a unique story to share given the life cycle of his or her organization and own skills and experience.

Discussion Questions

1. What leadership style is most effective in a museum going through a merger or other major change?
2. How would you go about developing a Succession Plan for your museum?
3. How are women making a difference as leaders in museums and nonprofits? What policies do you think the museum field should be considering in the wake of documented inequities in leadership diversity?

Notes

1. Peter Drucker, *Managing the Nonprofit Organization* (New York: HarperCollins, 1990), 20–27.
2. Ibid., 185.
3. Robert E. Kelley, "In Praise of Followership," *Harvard Business Review* 66, no. 6 (1988): 142–148.
4. This distinction was detailed in the work of Warren Bennis, *On Becoming a Leader* (New York: Addison Wesley, 1989).
5. Jim Collins, "Level 5 Leadership," *Harvard Business Review* 79, no. 1 (2001): 19–28.
6. Daniel Goleman, "What Makes a Leader?" *Harvard Business Review* 76, no. 6 (1998): 93–102.
7. Peter Senge, *The Fifth Discipline* (New York: Doubleday, 1990).
8. Michael Maccoby, "Narcissistic Leaders: The Inevitable Pros, the Inevitable Cons," *Harvard Business Review* (January–February 2000): 69–77.

9. Margarita Mayo, "If Humble People Make the Best Leaders, Why Do We Fall for Charismatic Narcissists," *Harvard Business Review* (April 2017), https://hbr.org/2017/04/if-humble-people-make-the-best-leaders-why-do -we-fall-for-charismatic-narcissists.

10. Jodi Kantor and David Strettfeld, "Inside Amazon: Wrestling Big Ideas in a Bruising Workplace," *New York Times*, August 15, 2015, https:// www.nytimes.com/2015/08/16/technology/inside-amazon-wrestling-big -ideas-in-a-bruising-workplace.html?_r=0.

11. Jena McGregor, "Expose at Uber Offers a Lesson of the Times," *Washington Post*, February 26, 2017, G1,4.

12. Daniel Goleman, "Leadership That Gets Results," *Harvard Business Review* 78, no. 2 (2000): 78–90.

13. Ronald Heifetz, Alexander Grahow, and Marty Linsky, "Leadership in a (Permanent) Crisis," *Harvard Business Review* 87, no. 7 (2009): 62–69.

14. Chip Heath and Dan Heath, *Decisive: How to Make Better Choices in Life and Work* (New York: Crown Business, 2013).

15. Boris Groysberg and Michael Slind, "Leadership Is a Conversation," *Harvard Business Review* 90, no. 6 (June 2012): 86–92.

16. Adi Ignatius, "Leadership with a Conscience," *Harvard Business Review* 93, no. 11 (2015): 50–63.

17. Elena L. Botelho, Kim R. Powell, Stephen Kincaid, and Dina Wang, "What Sets Successful CEOs Apart," *Harvard Business Review* 95, no. 3 (2017): 70–77.

18. Robert Janes, *Museums in a Troubled World* (New York: Routledge, 2009), 62–65.

19. Paul Redman, "A Great Garden of the World: Our Planning Story," in *The Manual of Strategic Planning for Cultural Organizations*, ed. Gail Dexter Lord and Kate Markert (Lanham, MD: Rowman & Littlefield, 2017), 139–144.

20. Sherene Suchy, "Emotional Intelligence, Passion and Museum Leadership," *Museum Management and Curatorship* 18, no. 1 (1999): 57–71.

21. Anne Ackerson and Joan Baldwin, *Leadership Matters* (Lanham, MD: AltaMira Press, 2014), 109–111.

22. Rebecca Koenig, "Many Nonprofits Lack Necessities of Sound Leadership," *Chronicle of Philanthropy*, March 15, 2016, https://www.philanthropy .com/article/Many-Nonprofits-Lack/235705.

23. Maria Cornelius, Rick Moyers, and Jeanne Bell, "Daring to Lead," Report by CompassPoint Nonprofit Services and the Meyer Foundation, July 2011, http://daringtolead.org.

24. Roger Shonfeld and Mariet Westermann, "Art Museum Staff Demographic Survey," Mellon Foundation, July 29, 2015, https://mellon .org/media/filer_public/ba/99/ba99e53a-48d5-4038-80e1-66f9ba1c020e/

awmf_museum_diversity_report_aamd_7-28-15.pdf and http://www.resnicow
.com/client-news/latest-study-gender-disparity-art-museum-directorships
-shows-gains-and-reversals-march.

25. Daniel Goleman, March 8, 2016, http://www.danielgoleman.info/
women-leaders-get-results-the-data/.

26. Sheryl Sandberg, *Lean In: Women, Work and the Will to Lead* (New
York: Alfred A. Knopf, 2013).

27. Jack Stripling, Katherine Mangan, and Brock Read, "After a Tumultu-
ous 7 Years, Teresa Sullivan Will Leave UVa," *Chronicle of Higher Education*,
January 23, 2017, http://www.chronicle.com/article/After-a-Tumultuous-7
-Years/238977.

28. Anne Midgette, "New President Deborah Rutter Is Kennedy Center's
Breath of Fresh Air from Windy City," *Washington Post*, August 28, 2014, https://
www.washingtonpost.com/entertainment/new-president-deborah-rutter-is
-kennedy-centers-breath-of-fresh-air-from-windy-city/2014/08/28/8381a600
-2c4c-11e4-9b98-848790384093_story.html?utm_term=.35e301e756c4.

29. Fred Plotkin, "How Deborah Rutter Manages," radio interview, May 21,
2016, http://www.wqxr.org/story/how-deborah-rutter-manages-conversation
-kennedy-center-president/.

30. P. McGlone, "Kennedy Center President Lures High Priced Stars
Yet Sparks an Exodus Among Senior Staff," *Washington Post*, July 18, 2017,
https://www.washingtonpost.com/entertainment/theater_dance/kennedy
-center-president-lures-high-priced-stars-yet-sparks-an-exodus-among
-senior-staff/2017/07/18/e9486c0e-5d9e-11e7-9b7d-.14576dc0f39d_story
.html?utm_campaign=buffer&utm_content=bufferb7126&utm_medium=
social&utm_source=twitter.com&utm_term=.4f0bc6a9f91f.

31. Peter Frumkin and Ana Kolendo, *Building for the Arts* (Chicago:
University of Chicago Press, 2014), 43–63.

32. Allison Weiss, "Relevance, Relationships, and Resources: The Three
R's of Museum Management," *History News* (Summer 2012): 7–16.

33. Author attended the session with Ellen Rosenthal, titled "Show Me
the Money," AAM Annual Meeting, Minneapolis, MN, May 1, 2012.

34. San Diego Museum of Man Strategic Plan, https://www.museumofman
.org/sites/default/files/sdmom_stratplan.pdf.

35. Robin Pogrebin, "Met Museum Changes Its Leadership Structure,"
New York Times, June 13, 2017, https://mobile.nytimes.com/2017/06/13/arts/
design/met-museum-changes-leadership-structure.html?smid=fb-share&
referer=http://m.facebook.com.

36. Richard W. Ferrin, *The Time Between* (Knoxville, TN: Wakefield
Connection, 2002).

37. Robert I. Goler, "Interim Directorship in Museums," in *Museum Management and Curatorship* 19, no. 4 (2004): 385–402.

38. Eben Harrell, "Succession Planning: What the Research Says," *Harvard Business Review* 94, no. 12 (2016): 71–74.

39. Peggy McGlone, "The Turnaround Artist," *Washington Post Magazine* (April 30, 2017): 32–36.

40. Charles F. Bryan Jr., "Stages in the Life of a Museum Director," *Museum News* (January–February 2007): 54–59.

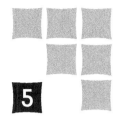

LEADERSHIP
AT ALL LEVELS

Leading from varied positions in the organization is common for most of us, for unless we work in complete isolation, we are working with supervisors, subordinates, and colleagues. The middle management function in organizations is absolutely essential for success. These individuals coordinate work, set standards, manage others, build and spend budgets, and advocate for best practices. Communication is a critical skill. The work of middle management is often overlooked as routine, but these individuals have a lot of power to make things happen. Without their buy-in and focused attention, very little significant work will be done. While these individuals are facilitators and enablers, they can also be obstructionists. Since most museum staff will find themselves at this level of the organization it is critical to examine how this function serves as an important part of the leadership system. This chapter will define the role of middle management and examine how these individuals impact the change process, and how this role demonstrates an important aspect of leadership in museums. Although we are looking at middle managers it is clear that some smaller museums will not have layers of staff, thus we are talking about individuals below the director or CEO level.

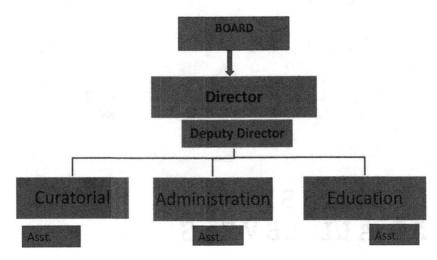

Figure 5.1. Hierarchical organization.
Courtesy of the author.

The Middle Manager Defined

Figure 5.1 illustrates the typical hierarchical structure highlighting the middle manager's placement. Who are the middle managers? In most organizations they will be department heads, standing committee members, project managers, and even the deputy director. Middle managers may be members of a senior team or serve at a lower level. They serve as valuable players in the organization for the following reasons:

- They generate good ideas.
- They control resources and can implement change.
- They can be seen as positive critics.
- They have informal power.
- They understand the morale issues of the staff.
- They can serve as positive role models.

This level of the organization breeds leaders. Because they know the business and gain expertise through their work, they are often seen as rising stars. Despite all these positives the role can be loaded with frustration and challenges. In knowledge-intensive industries (including museums) the middle manager is often the project manager leading the team of creative and other specialists. In fact in most industries the details of how work is done is left to managers at the middle. Studies of creative work such as computer game design have shown that innovators are only as good as the performance of their managers. A lot of responsibility![1]

Despite these findings, corporate middle management has been described as a thankless job. In the experience of many organizations undergoing retrenchment, reorganization, or mergers and takeovers, the middle manager is often a victim. Cutting jobs to save money and subsequently reorganizing to consolidate functions may squeeze the role into nonexistence or add a whole new set of responsibilities. For years the middle manager has been viewed as a bureaucrat defending their turf. Often when communicating with higher ups they feel that their good ideas are ignored. But in the modern world of constant change the middle manager deserves a new level of respect. In a time of radical change the middle manager can play the following roles:

- Entrepreneur: creating ideas on how to change
- Communicator: interpreting the details of change
- Therapist: ameliorate the levels of fear among staff
- Tightrope artist: balancing change and continuity

Seeking the best people to complete this critical work requires that organizations hire, groom, and prepare managers for this role. Often the types of people who should be singled out are those who are fearless in regard to change. Who has volunteered to help? Who are the "positive critics" on the staff? Who has "informal power" and influence as a respected peer? How self-aware are these people? Do they believe in the mission?[2]

So top leadership needs to nurture these people. Middle managers need to serve as strong advocates for their staff, assure clear understanding and alignment with organizational goals, and be exceptional communicators. They must spend time on building trust of higher-level executives, and create coalitions with colleagues across the organization. As the middle manager is close to the execution of programs, they may also serve to raise the flag about problems. The classic whistle-blower is someone with high expectations for ethical behavior and believes deeply in the operating values of their organization. Unfortunately, the downside of middle management is that whistle blowing can result in negative consequences. Sometimes in the form of retaliation. Importantly, middle managers are 360-degree experts. They need to attract, hire, and orient their subordinate staff or project team members; they need to establish work standards in line with professional policies and expectations; and they need to manage the dreams and desires of their staff, peers, and leaders. At the same time they need to acquire and utilize resources responsibly and assure that goals and objectives are met on time.

Leading Change from the Middle

Establishing the importance of the middle manager leads to the process of change. At all levels of the organization there are individuals charged with implementing change through formal assignment from senior management. But, there can be significant change bubbling up from all levels of the organization. In her landmark book on *Tempered Radicals*, Debra Myerson lays out case studies of changes at the middle. In these cases individuals take small steps to initiate change in the organization based on observations of problems that need resolution. Often individuals at lower levels are likely to see the problem long before top leadership is aware of it. These "everyday leaders" work slowly to shake up the status quo while being conscious of their self-preservation. Thus despite the problematic situation, they tolerate the status quo while advancing small wins. Examples include middle managers who make changes within their own office that improve the morale of staff, such as allowing staff to have alternative work schedules. Sometimes these changes although modest are not in line with the operating culture of the business. This could then result in criticism from peers. Working within the system is the premise that allows these individuals to survive. Internal change agents might include individuals organizing appeals to management, for example to seek adoption of new technology or creation of new policies. Often ethical concerns will be an issue. For example, curatorial staff at the Museum of American History spoke out in opposition to outside donor interference in exhibition development. These varied voices were loud enough for the senior management to eventually address the issue of policy in dealing with donations. This collective action is different from an individual effort and may take more time to craft given the number of participants in the group. Another example is the emerging museum professionals groups or those representing rights and concerns of museum workers addressing pay issues and those of diversity and inclusion. Not existing as sanctioned groups they need to realize their influence over change will take longer and perhaps be more frustrating and discouraging than that of a group that has been formally appointed by the organization. The everyday leader needs to build networks of sympathetic peers relying on a culture of respect.[3]

Teaming

Looking at other examples in the museum field, consider how cross-functional teams can serve to influence the change process. Working as tempered radicals these team efforts can also create the scenario needed to solve fundamental problems. An example is an unsanctioned group at a museum that took it upon themselves to seek solutions to the allocation of space to accommodate growing collections, renovations, and changing exhibitions. This group was composed of collections managers, registrars, facilities managers, and curators. They worked collaboratively on creating a matrix of spaces, and projected needs to serve programs and exhibitions. With the diligent work of this group senior management soon recognized the value of the improvements being made and sanctioned their work over the following ten-year period of renovation and reinstallation. Other examples of quiet change from the middle include the work done by various professionals in support of building standards and best practices among a network of museums such as the AAM Educator's Committee.

The importance of teaming is critical for making change work at the middle of the organization. Putting a team together for a problem-solving session as noted above is one example. Teams can also serve as standing committees working collaboratively to make decisions about programs or policies, such as a committee that reviews ideas for new exhibitions. Where the members see each other as "customers" there can be an even greater level of respect and understanding. Mutual accountability allows for a more open process of communications and problem solving.

In other ways we need to look at the composition of our teams. Clearly teams should be representative of needed skills and interested stakeholders. Skills in order to assure that the work will be successful. Stakeholders to assure that the process will be accepted by those who might oppose the idea. One way to do this is to "include your enemies" on the team. Enemies may seem like too strong a word, but individuals who are rivals or who simply do not agree on much often may need to collaborate. Building a trusting relationship with this type of colleague can be daunting. This is important because working together to solve a problem will be of benefit to both individual staff development and achieving mission. Thinking about Senge's "mental models" we may see in these teams a bias against a certain individual or job category. A classic in the museum field would be the role of the conservator who may frequently criticize exhibition design ideas or activities that could harm collections. The staff member with the opposing viewpoint is very likely going to be someone with influence and value. Middle managers are in a position to see the reality of museum operations and if they value the mission then their input should not be rejected by senior leaders. The museum should value truth as opposed to encouraging "yes people" that may be echoing what they think senior management wants to hear. These "no people" can often be tapped to lead task forces or other problem-solving groups in search of innovative solutions.[4] As a follow-up to the issue of opposing views on teams, this also allows one to value diversity and to recognize the strengths of people not like you. A project team leader might be inclined to ask their trusted or admired colleagues to join their team because they think alike or at a minimum their loyalty will be unquestioned. However, the organization that believes in diversity and inclusion is wise to move away from this approach.

Communication Style

Communication style is an important factor in leading a change movement at all levels, but in particular when the individual is not in a power position. Adam Grant writing in *Give and Take* described the value of a "powerless" approach to communications. This is simply a modest and self-effacing style. Signaling vulnerability this type of communication relies on seeking advice and opinions of others, asking questions instead of making definitive statements, assuring others that you are not perfect through telling a story about your foibles, or revealing a mistake that tells others you are human. This approach then transfers the power to the listener. Research has shown that seeking advice is most effective when we lack authority, which is often the case with middle managers.[5]

Other options for communications upward (and across) include analyzing the learning style of superiors in order to effectively get your message across. Since everyone tends to have differing styles it can be a real challenge to do this. Observation of the individual over time allows a lower level employee to understand these styles. For example, a charismatic leader will usually prefer ideas that are exciting and results-oriented. They do not want to be presented with details. On the other hand, a leader who tends to be skeptical or controlling in their style will no doubt expect to be presented with outside opinions and a lot of detailed data. Other leaders tend to be cautious and will be comfortable only following ideas that have been successfully implemented by others. Clearly there are other types of learning styles and personality profiles that will require the middle manager to be thoughtful in their messaging.[6]

What other tips are needed to assure the staff member at the middle provides leadership? Sometimes it is best to think boldly about new ideas. Volunteering for big projects shows that you are interested in advancing the agenda of the organization. In all cases give proper credit to the boss, peers, and subordinates. Be realistic in your expectations. Most importantly, since many leaders are very busy it's easy to assume they know what you are doing. They are not privy to all the details of the organization, but you can help them by keeping them informed. When seeking approval for a new idea, be persistent but not annoying. Sometimes you have to look for the right moment to share your ideas. Most emphatically, do not allow the boss to be surprised. The middle manager should be working to build confidence and trust from peers, subordinates, and upper management. Assuring that you can be trusted to make a solid contribution to the work of the organization allows for greater success at all levels.

Multiple bosses can be a nightmare. However, this is pretty common. Consider the fact that the CEO works for a board of directors or trustees. In this case many individuals serve as the boss. So although most employees have one boss, there are layers of senior management and the board to consider. How do you manage this? Probably through frequent face-to-face communications. Keeping everyone informed is critical. Let them all know what you are recommending. Meet in person when you can as that can do much to avoid misunderstandings and it shows respect. Don't be afraid to copy all parties on your email communications. Frequently there is an executive team that you need to involve as you make a case for your idea. Pursuing a change initiative should include informing all these players, not just your boss. Other ways you may be confronting multiple bosses is through the matrix structure common in project management. Employees can be subject to the supervision of both a functional manager and project manager. In this instance workers commonly will have time management and priority work conflicts as well as a tendency to get overwhelmed. If the two managers do not agree or coordinate on their expectations, the staff member may be set up for failure. Being aware of these issues is critical. In the end determining who will be the ultimate decision maker when it comes to performance reviews and long-term assignments is most important. Thus it's up to the individual worker to seek clarifications on priorities, to keep all supervisors informed about their workload, and to set boundaries to avoid getting overloaded. Clearly making these changes from the middle requires knowing your museum, engaging the staff that will be in your cohort, contributing your skills, emphasizing collaboration, seeking innovation, and being reliable and indispensable. Underlying this is the factor of ambiguity and the sometimes slow pace of change.

Strategies for Leading Up in Museums

The Number Two or Deputy Role

As we have seen throughout this chapter there are varied ways of making your ideas heard and succeeding in your interaction with the senior management. The role of the deputy director is a unique opportunity for leadership. This position is often one that functions as a chief operating officer, but could also serve as a head of museum programs. The deputy may also end up serving as acting director or

interim when needed. As these individuals work closely on a regular basis the deputy should be someone with complementary skills
and styles. Often the charismatic and visionary director would seek a
strong administrator as deputy.

In many cases the deputy lacks power and must operate with personal influence and detailed knowledge of the museum's priorities. The
second in command is often an awkward role as other senior staff may
bypass them in order to work directly with the CEO. Certain attributes
will lead to success in this role. Not being concerned about your ego
is one. It is important to be comfortable with the fact that you will not
get all the credit. Working from behind the scenes is often expected of
a deputy who will be building networks and listening to individuals
throughout the organization about day-to-day operations. One key
role of this individual is to let the boss know when they have made a
mistake, or in a more proactive role, to advise on making the best decisions. Museum consultants John Durel and Will Phillips wrote a per-
ceptive guidebook for the deputy director. The role is not one size fits
all. They interviewed a number of deputies and found that they have
many key roles such as gatekeeper, confidant, strategist, and key partner. Some were tasked with managing the strategic planning process
and its implementation working closely with other senior staff. Many
noted that they often acted as advisors to other staff, which demanded
discretion and good facilitation skills when presented with problems.
Often they operated in an atmosphere of ambiguity as far as authority is concerned. Of interest is that 50 percent of the individuals they
interviewed were not sure they wanted to rise to the CEO spot. When
we further examine the middle manager in museums we will see why
that is not a surprising finding.[7]

Working from the Middle

Museums have two types of middle management: the project manager
and the functional manager. The distinction between these two roles
lies in the amount of formal authority they have in regard to resources
such as staff and funds. In writing about the function of middle management in museums, Maria Quinlin Leiby noted in her experience
and that of others she interviewed for her *History News* article, that
the value of middle management is in keeping you close to the work

you love. Although there are downsides to supervising, budgeting, reporting and negotiating there is still a hands on connection to the basic functions that attracted us to the field: collections care, research, education, and other public-facing activities. Often individuals at the middle are really not interested in serving as senior leaders, being more than happy that someone above them is making the hard decisions. Even at this level though individuals need to hone their skills as communicators and other functions of management.[8] A case study of a staff member who moved into a department head position is that of Rafael Rosa in taking on the role of vice president of education at the Chicago Academy of Sciences where he managed a staff of twenty. He was promoted to this position after sixteen years as an educator. Despite solid experience in his field he felt unprepared for the challenge of becoming a department head. In an honest assessment he pointed to his lack of management experience, but deep knowledge of programs. There were areas where he felt unprepared, for example in running public programs and in working with teen audiences. He quickly learned that his staff knew more than he did in certain areas. Thus the need to trust in his subordinates. Other challenges were those associated with budget, advocacy of museum wide programs with his staff, and feeling lonely—he was no longer a peer, but the boss. His solution was to seek advice from peers outside the museum, to work more closely with the CFO on budgeting, and actively employ his staff in department decision making.[9]

The Project Manager or Team Leader's Role

The role of project manager is a now considered one of the most important middle management roles. Much has been written about the unique nature of this position, which is part manager and part leader. This is not a purely supervisory or coordinating position on the team, but one that brings together the resources allocated to produce the desired product within time, on budget and with a sense of celebration on the part of all involved. Not every museum has dedicated project managers, but frequently a knowledgeable functional staff member will be assigned this role. That individual will still need to play a coordinating role among peers and others. So no matter what the title, the skills are often the same. In very large projects such as an expansion or renovation it is not unusual to hire an outside expert to run the project. The downside of this decision might be their lack of understanding of the museum business and even a lack of dedication to the mission and values of the museum. The selection of a project manager for large and complex initiatives requires a good deal of consideration. For example a museum may appoint a senior staff member to oversee the development and implementation of a major reinstallation. Or perhaps they will select a seasoned consultant to join the museum to help them through the project. In either case the level of trust in the individual's understanding of the museum's culture and goals is critical.[10]

Project managers are the ones charged with advocating for the project, the team process, and handling numerous stakeholders with varying work styles and expectations.[11] Team dynamics can be a constant challenge and one aspect of managing projects that requires finesse. One of the most important functions of the project manager is building the team. This requires good working relations with both team members and functional managers. Project managers negotiate with functional office heads for the time of their staff. There is no authority in this role so that skills of communication and influence are paramount.

There are two main responsibilities for the project manager: administration and leadership. Obviously the administrative role involves securing staff and contract support, building the team, scheduling, budgeting, milestone review, meeting management, reporting on progress, and handling the flow of information among the many individuals invested in the project itself. Project managers have to *know* the business, understanding the tasks and costs, and be aware of operating policies and procedures. They may need to hire new staff and negotiate contracts. Monitoring progress involves frequent milestone reviews and formal reporting on the status of the project to senior management and the museum board. They are the corporate memory of the project and manage all documentation. Their leadership function is more complex. It involves building a high performing team, providing training and positive feedback, monitoring group morale, listening to stakeholders, keeping open communications at all levels of the organization, resolving conflict, and solving problems. Clearly these are all difficult tasks and not everyone is capable of meeting these expectations.

Challenges abound in this role. Poorly identified needs can lead to cost overruns or rework. Poor planning and controls, inability to influence teams or higher-level management can derail the project. Often project managers are handling two or three major projects at once or running projects plus ongoing functional work. Therefore, savvy project managers need to work with discipline and speed to anticipate problems in advance and get below the surface to examine hidden agendas of team members. Being flexible and risk-averse are two perhaps opposing traits. Things will go wrong and the project manager needs to know how to work the system through their personal persuasion if not formal authority. One-on-one meetings and informal reviews by checking in on the team can be a confidence building approach. The reality is that the team is a temporary entity, and the project manager has limited authority. Often the project will be assigned a senior management sponsor (say a vice president for collections) who will work to assure that the project manager has support at a higher level when needed. However, the power of the project manager should emanate from their ability to influence the team through trust building, helping them resolve time management or technical problems, and providing positive feedback and recognition. A high level of maturity and sensitivity to individual concerns is important along with a strong understanding of the museum's values and standards of production.

Many times people are tapped for this job without any formal training. They thus learn on the job and over time may become very proficient. Serving as a conduit between staff and management is also a unique function. They have a great deal of knowledge about the organization and its weaknesses and strengths as they have a unique view of several functions. What lessons they have learned are passed on informally to others in the organization.[12] In conversations with museum project managers the author has learned that the challenges of their assignments require consistent attention to detail, including contract negotiation, budget and timeline adjustments, team meetings, advocacy to senior management for resources, and conflict resolution within the team. Frequently they must meet one on one with functional office managers to resolve problems. Switching from a focus on the functional work of their department to a cross-functional team's end goals can be daunting. Thus people who are selected for these assignments are often highly productive individuals given an opportunity to lead and learn on the job. An example is the work of technology staff in developing a new website for a small museum. Team leadership involves running a series of workshops to design the website including input from several functional offices including curatorial. Designing a website involves new ways of writing and user-centered design solutions. These approaches can be foreign to traditional curatorial staff and thus involve more diplomacy and team learning than a traditional exhibition, for example. Project managers need to be alert to hidden agendas, fears, and goals of their teams.

An interesting example of a middle management team was the transition group that worked on the opening of the new National Museum of the American Indian in 2004. This group of middle management staff coordinated the planning and execution of the opening events including exhibition installations, storage, staffing, and special events. In this case and similar instances there is a temporary structure in place that dissolves at the opening of the museum. Managing the process is very much a matter of using influence, not power.

Beyond the team, there is the all-important interface with higher management. How do project managers share information and influence decision makers at different levels of the organization? In larger museums they may need to work with functional managers of departments as well as the director and board. Higher-level managers are less likely to want a lot of detail so a one-sheet summary of the project work may suffice. There is value in having a meeting of the entire team with senior management. This can build confidence in the work of the team and improve morale of staff involved. Leading up involves a whole set of skills. One thing that is important is to spend some time understanding the way that senior managers like to receive information. As mentioned above regarding communications there may be a learning style that will need to be considered as the project manager works with senior staff. They may need to enlist the support of the multiple bosses at the top who can serve as allies depending on the issue at stake. The CEO may prefer that your project update be made to the entire senior team, including written and oral reports, especially if you need to influence a decision about resources or other major issues.

If the middle manager has bad news, the first rule is always present options for resolving the problem. Many leaders prefer to have options rather than to make a decision with insufficient information. Allies or expert opinions are also very useful in this situation. You may need to build a coalition among colleagues or other managers to assure that the museum leader is comfortable. If you are in a position to disagree with a top manager, then you may need to ask permission to present an opposing position, be sure to use facts and not judgments, be humble, show respect, and link your position to the good of the museum. Delivering the message with diplomacy and care is important, as is being honest with the facts that can lead to success or failure of the project.[13] The Smithsonian Institution has launched an internal leadership training program for middle management staff. Over a period of one year, individuals selected for the program have the opportunity to learn best practices in leadership, practice working in cross-functional teams, and learn communications skills. They are also provided a senior staff mentor who works with them on a variety of projects serving as an informal coach. This training provides these staff members with the skills and personal courage to communicate clearly with senior managers, even when the news is bad. Speaking truth to power can be a risky endeavor. Creating a set of optional solutions to assist in working through the problems and enlisting allies to vouch for the facts is critical. Another part of the middle management training included conflict management skills.[14]

An interesting example of middle management change is the work at the Santa Cruz Museum of Art and History. Working with senior management, staff here were eager to build a participative culture in planning and implementing programs. The practice of crowdsourcing exhibition and program ideas along with the inevitable power shift to the community was a unique and risky venture. This phenomenon was detailed in director Nina Simon's *Participatory Museum* text. The reality of making a radical change, in line with the vision of the executive director is a test for middle managers. Resistance to participatory planning has been well documented. A major change can upend the professional status of staff members and confuse all players. What are the rules? Is this just a fad? Loss of control is one major concern. As this is a new way of operating, the affected staff need to be in control of the process. Starting small is always a good way to introduce new approaches as we learned in chapter 3 on organizational change. Assigning a trusted middle manager to the role of coordinating work with community groups is a way to build confidence in the new approach. Implementing new approaches works well when the museum begins with small experiments, puts money into these new initiatives, and develops complementary policies. Encouraging new ideas from the bottom up empowers staff in the new approaches. And giving staff credit for the success of these efforts is paramount.[15]

In fact an important option for experimenting in a museum is establishing a rapid prototyping team that can be charged with developing solutions to important problems or to define new ways of doing their work in a reengineering effort. This type of middle management planning is not the customary approach for museums, but in the volatile world it will soon become a necessity. The outcome is understanding that your colleagues' work is as important as yours. You are both working toward achieving the goals of the organization. A pitfall of the experimental team is the issue of boundaries and how they can inhibit productive communications. For example when newly formed teams are working on a problem individuals may be reluctant to share information that is unique and helpful as they fear being rejected. Differences in status may cause this. A collections manager may defer to the curator's views because of their background, title, or education. Other differences can become a problem including gender and race. In cases where this occurs there can be unwillingness to share information that can be a breakthrough in problem solving. Thus the need of the middle manager in charge to be able to facilitate a fruitful dialogue.

Profiles of Museum Departmental Leaders

A few examples of successful middle managers will help to illustrate what can be done at this level. Anne Ackerson and Joan Baldwin were fortunate to include middle managers in their pool of interviewees for the text *Leadership Matters*. One such example is that of Ryan Spencer, who in 2014 was manager of Firestone Farm and Equine Operations at The Henry Ford. His profile is one of an enthusiastic and dedicated manager who believes in group learning and an adherence to the mission of the museum on a daily basis. He exhibits an amazing dedication to the team and as a result their work adds value to the museum.[16]

There are other examples of leaders at the department level of museums. In chapter 8 the stories of three functional managers making a difference are featured. Making a major contribution to the mission of her museum is Jillian Jones at the Albright-Knox Art Gallery in Buffalo, New York. As director of advancement and as a member of the senior leadership team, she coordinated efforts to secure a significant capital campaign gift in support of a new expansion project. Her role in the museum includes working with the senior team to revitalize the work of the museum to focus on public engagement, diversity, and innovation. Jones moved from a middle manager position in her previous job to senior management at Albright-Knox, which required new approaches to organizational design and internal communications. The work of Lauren Shenfeld at the EdVenture Children's Museum in Columbia, South Carolina, is another example of departmental leadership. Her role has included strategic planning, training for front line staff, and with the museum's CEO revising the values of the museum to reflect the museum's operational philosophy. Shenfeld found that leading this change at the middle was challenging including a reorganization of her department, as is often the case when a transformation is underway. The work of Sandra Smith at the Heinz History Center in Pittsburgh focuses on public engagement. Her role has allowed for prototyping new approaches to programming at the museum. She shares their story of success. Each case study details the personal reflections of these individuals as leaders.

Finally, in considering the issue of leading up, the director of the museum is also in a position to influence and successfully communicate with the board of trustees and other important decision makers. Many of the approaches mentioned above will be useful to the chief executive as well as other staff. It is critical to examine twenty-first-century views on innovative organizational structures, transformative change initiatives, and the way that leaders at all levels adapt to internal and external changes.

Discussion Questions

1. How does your museum utilize project management systems to train staff in leadership skills?
2. Consider ways in which a difficult problem can be resolved through collaboration across the organization.

3. How do museum staff work as "tempered radicals" in small museums?

4. How does the CEO or director influence change in working with the board?

Notes

1. Ethan Mollick, "Why Middle Managers May Be the Most Important People in Your Company," *Knowledge at Wharton*, May 25, 2011, http://knowledge.wharton.upenn.edu/article/why-middle-managers-may-be-the-most-important-people-in-your-company/.

2. Quy Nguyen Huy, "In Praise of Middle Managers," *Harvard Business Review* 79, no. 8 (2001): 72–79.

3. Debra E. Meyerson, *Tempered Radicals: How Everyday Leaders Inspire Change at Work* (Boston: Harvard Business School Publishing, 2003), 165–171.

4. Robert Janes, *Museums without Borders* (London: Routledge, 2016), 179.

5. Adam Grant, *Give and Take* (New York: Viking Press, 2013), 150.

6. Gary A. Williams and Robert B. Miller, "Change the Way You Persuade," *Harvard Business Review* 80, no. 5 (May 2002): 64–73.

7. John Durel and Will Phillips, *The Deputy's Handbook* (n.p.: Qm^2, 2002).

8. Maria Quinlan Leiby, "Choosing Middle Management," *History News* 58, no. 4 (2003): 13–14.

9. Rafael Rosa, "Welcome, Mr. Director, and Good Luck!" *Journal of Museum Education* 34, no. 2 (Summer 2009): 129–138.

10. Walter Crimm, Martha Morris, and L. Carole Wharton, *Planning Successful Museum Building Projects* (Lanham, MD: AltaMira Press), 43.

11. Polly McKenna-Cress and Janet Kamien, *Creating Exhibitions* (New York: John Wiley and Sons, 2013), 194.

12. David Frame, *Managing Projects in Organizations* (New York: Wiley, 2003), 69–70.

13. Amy Gallo, "How to Disagree with Someone More Powerful Than You," *Harvard Business Review*, March 2016, https://hbr.org/2016/03/how-to-disagree-with-someone-more-powerful-than-you?platform=hootsuite.

14. Author conversation with Lauren Telchin-Katz, participant in the Russell E. Palmer Leadership Development Program at the Smithsonian.

15. Nina Simon, *The Participatory Museum* (Santa Cruz, CA: Museum 2.0, 2010), 321–347.

16. Anne W. Ackerson and Joan H. Baldwin, *Leadership Matters* (Lanham, MD: AltaMira Press, 2014), 78–81.

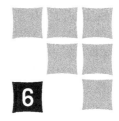

LEADERSHIP FOR THE FUTURE

INNOVATION

Leadership success today and in the future requires an arsenal of approaches. These include innovation and change, decision making and planning, design thinking and agile project management, internal restructuring and team processes, as well as new business models and technology solutions. This chapter will look at the best practices in business and nonprofit leadership and highlight successful museum cases studies. Transformational and entrepreneurial leaders will be featured.

Innovation: Process and Structure

The idea of innovation is a core value in our century. The modern world is the result of hundreds of innovations in all sectors. Museum innovation is blooming in the twenty-first century with an almost religious fervor. Taking a closer look at what we mean by this activity will help to define how it is used to drive success. Chapter 3 examined the theory of "disruptive" innovation in organizations as first defined in the mid-1990s. The theory notes that start-up companies enter markets to serve segments that have unmet needs. As they grow they may advance to outpace incumbent organizations by gaining larger and larger market share. Apple's iPhone was considered a disrupter as it offered desktop/laptop functions in a mobile format. In most cases disruptive innovation is a process that unfolds over time, and does not produce immediate change. The genesis of this leadership philosophy lies in the Total Quality Management (TQM) movement made popular in the US in the 1980s. Based on a theory of continuous improvement, customer focus, and employee involvement, TQM led to new workplace collaboration between workers and managers in manufacturing and service industries. A well-known example was the New United Motor Manufacturing, Inc. (NUMMI) auto plant in California where Japanese systems of TQM revolutionized the role of the worker as decision maker resulting in streamlined process and improved production quality.[1]

Who are the innovators today? In writing about this phenomenon in his best-selling book *Originals* Adam Grant notes that it's not always the vocal visionary that leads change. In fact successful innovators tend to move more slowly to avoid failure. "They are the ones who reluctantly tiptoe to the edge of a cliff, calculate the rate of descent, triple-check their parachutes, and set up a safety net at the bottom just in case."[2] Procrastination is a virtue in this scenario, given the power of divergent thinking where small tweaks over time can lead to a more robust idea. Innovators toss out ideas and seek feedback. In the workplace that is often from colleagues. Originals are more successful in fostering change through exercise of influence; consider the "powerless communication" of "tempered radicals" as discussed in chapter 5. One of the downsides of sustaining the creative spirit in organizations is as they mature on the life cycle they tend to value complacency. Therefore, it is important for leaders to consistently encourage a diversity of ideas and approaches.

Innovation places emphasis on risk and failure. Thus the contemporary leader needs to create an atmosphere that will encourage and protect staff as they try new approaches. Most individuals resist experimenting as failure is unpleasant and undermines self-confidence. Smart leaders will make it safe by emphasizing a culture of learning. Encouraging and perhaps rewarding failure as long as it provides lessons is a good approach. The leader should "adopt an inquiry orientation that reflects curiosity, patience, and a tolerance for ambiguity."[3] Leaders need to be open to new ideas. Effective leaders seek brutal honesty from their stakeholders and staff, breaking down barriers that are often erected around the CEO function. Happy talk is a huge deterrent to understanding threats. Innovation always involves at least an implicit acknowledgment that you were wrong about something before.

Learning Organizations as Innovators

The most important consideration for innovation in organizations is to assure there is a process in place for enterprise-wide learning. Reasons why this might not happen include fear of failure, over-reliance on past performance, dependence on outside experts, and eagerness to try too many new things. Importantly then leaders need to emphasize that failures are learning opportunities and individuals need to own their mistakes. In a stressed and fast-paced world there is not sufficient time for employees to stop and reflect, so taking breaks and vacations is critical. Leaders who are successful set aside time to think. There is no set formula for this, but it should be done. For example, one might have a rule that there can be no meetings on Fridays in order for staff to be reflective. The over-reliance on outside expertise rings true with museums as they often bring in consultants. While this can be invigorating, it could also be a potential trap. The people who are on the front lines are very likely the best source of data and problem solving, not necessarily the opinions of an outside expert. Think of the front-line value of Nordstrom's sales force empowered to solve problems immediately.[4]

Innovation and the Agile Approach

What is Agile? This is a popular system for software development in service industries including an increasing number of museums. The process involves small cross-disciplinary teams that work as a "scrum." They employ creative and adaptive teamwork in solving complex problems. The goal is to continually eliminate wasted time and steps characteristic of a traditional methodology. Streamlining operations helps to speed decision making and reduce the need for costly and time-consuming development time. Small groups (the scrums) work on parts of the problem. They resolve disagreements through experimentation and feedback rather than endless debates or appeals to authority. They test small working prototypes of part or all of the products with a few customers. Feedback is built into the product on a cyclical basis. Agile requires engaging team members from across the disciplines, and thus provides an internal staff development opportunity as well as trust building. This is a new approach to developing programs and museums are beginning to apply this beyond the software arena.[5] Writing in *Museum* magazine Elizabeth Merritt describes the agile design process as one that favors "small bets" toward learning and along the way accepts failures as learning tools. So we need to discard the "culture of perfection" in order to learn from mistakes. A culture of learning and continuous improvement has been embraced by the most successful organizations in the corporate sector for several decades. Yet it is still not a comfortable fit in many museums. Fortunately, the Institute of Museum and Library Services (IMLS) has begun to offer funding for "spark" grants for those small programs that advance a new approach to twenty-first-century skill building.[6]

Rapid prototyping can lead to breakthroughs in serving new audiences. Sharing these success stories more widely is an imperative. Blogs such as Design Thinking for Museums.net provide a useful forum. A museum embracing the agile approach is the Getty. Featured case studies include exhibition signage, web page redesign, and educational programs. Each project illustrates brainstorming and a prototyping approach with feedback loops from end users and audiences.[7]

Related to the agile approach is design thinking. Perhaps the most interesting similarity is that in both methodologies staff are the drivers of projects and change. Both organize employees in cross-functional teams that stimulate solutions for a product, service, or software. The agile approach is usually employed in software projects while design thinking is used more broadly in project development. Reframing the description of a problem, using prototyping, and open-ended "what if" questions are the typical tools. Visualizations, flow charts, and storytelling are often a part of the process as is working with a diversity of voices both within and outside the organization. A classic use of design thinking in museums is the development of new exhibitions. But it could also work for reengineering a facilities process, or developing a new strategic plan. It is a powerful approach to managing change but adds an important dimension in "deep interaction with stakeholders," in this case, the customer. Design thinking is "human-centered" and embodies empathy, exploration, and iteration; small steps to reach the right solution. For museums this type of approach is most often used in developing a better understanding of the needs of communities, and in so doing helping to solve a social problem. Examples might include improved environmental sustainability programs or ways to increase more healthful eating among schoolchildren. In all cases the power of diversity is emphasized; that is, including many voices in the process.[8]

Museums have embraced design thinking in important ways. The Grand Rapids Art Museum is using this approach in many of their activities, not just exhibitions. Staff received special training in these techniques to assure success in a variety of endeavors. As museums need to be responsive to external change, the design thinking approach will help in creating prototypes for more nimble changing exhibitions.[9] This approach is gaining strength and importance. San Francisco's Exploratorium recently appointed Chris Flink, an IDEO designer, as executive director. The museum has been known for valuing experimentation and this step will assure that an innovative leader is in place to guide their programs.[10]

Rethinking Structures

The creative process cannot thrive in a traditional organizational structure as is clear from the discussion above. Therefore, we need to banish territoriality, silos, and hierarchies. Changing organizational structures is imperative but not easy. Some of these solutions are radical while others tinker with the system through temporary changes. There are two ways to define this change: one is restructuring and the other is reconfiguration. The former is often more dramatic with new units and staff assignments that reflect the core business activities. Traditionally this is the favored approach. However, in a volatile world the application of quick small-scale changes may make the most sense. This is in line with the theory of adaptive leadership discussed in chapter 4. Basically, the organization will employ a team-based approach to the implementation of core work.

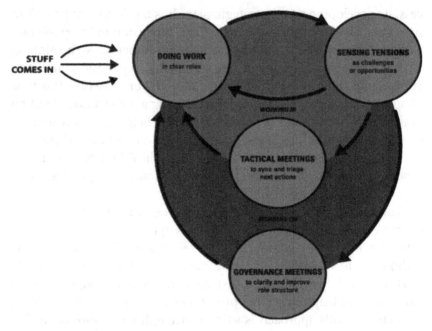

Figure 6.1. Holacracy chart.
Courtesy holacracy.org.

In recent years there has been a growing emphasis on the self-managed (or "egoless") team environment, called Holacracy. These are popular structures that foster innovation, flexibility, and productivity. And very likely go nicely with the agile and design thinking systems mentioned above. In Holacracy structures called "circles" attempt to do away with traditional hierarchy (see figure 6.1). Staff move in and out of the circles as needed to complete work. Teams design their work and govern themselves with formal written pledges to detail mutual accountability. Decisions are made by consensus. Staff members may have more than one role in these circles that emphasize a multi-skilled approach. These types of teams form and disband and redefine individual roles in response to the needs of the organization.[11] In fact, some organizations are forgoing hiring permanent staff for the practice of creating "on-demand teams," which are composed of consultants, freelancers, and specialists. The value of this approach is that the teams draw on skilled experts instead of existing staff that may not be trained for the specialized work. This allows the organization to move quickly in a competitive world and ideally save money on employee overhead costs. The contemporary workforce is changing and recent surveys show that individuals might prefer this "on-demand" type of work experience over permanent employment.[12] Would this work for museums? Perhaps only in start-ups or in museums with a mandate to work with intense levels of innovation. One major criticism of self-managed teams is the lack of coordination, detail development, advocacy, and conflict resolution skills of a strong project manager. For example, in applying new modes of project work Google found that employing leaders who develop and motivate their team and share information effectively was important in a culture of highly independent engineers. All these "soft" skills were critical to revising their work structures. And this was reinforced by feedback surveys from employees.[13]

No matter what structure is selected the process of restructuring can be time-consuming and painful. As we discussed in chapter 3 on managing change, reorganization is a consistent activity in most sectors. Reorganizations require a great deal of persuasion as staff often see this as just another change mandated by management. Often reorganizations result in the wrong people being assigned to power positions. Existing relationships are impacted and staff are uncertain about their roles. A strong mandate for change is needed to kick-start the restructuring. Sadly, some changes are not well thought out let alone well received. Including the voices of staff, assigning a project manager, and excellent communications can help smooth the way. From a small change to a major upheaval such as a merger, close attention to planning and implementation are needed along with systems to seek feedback and share information. There should be no surprises when a change is announced, yet frequently management overlooks the need to keep people in the loop and explain the decision criteria. Failure of reorganizations occurs due to employee resistance, insufficient time and money invested in the implementation, distraction of staff, senior manager resistance, and work processes remaining the same. There should always be a personal connection as changes are being made. The example of the American History Museum case in chapter 3 highlights ways that reorganizations can be managed with respect for staff.

Reengineering existing processes can also be another way to tweak the structure without a major reorganization. An example is that of the Canadian Museum of History, which with 4,000,000 artifacts and a staff of 400 underwent several major changes including a name change and partnerships with other museums. One major goal was to redefine working relationships among staff involved in the "experience development process." Under the leadership of their Project Management Office this effort involved a team of fifteen middle managers working together to dissect and redesign the workflow. An iterative process not unlike agile design systems allowed for testing of ideas among users and making adjustments along the way in a nonlinear and interactive approach. The result was an exhibition development system with clearer role definition, distributed authority, shorter time frames, and more accountability among the management team.[14]

Aside from reengineering, prototyping, and other modern systems how can we streamline the decision process? Roadblocks to organizational change often include time-wasting meetings. They can slow down the process and drive staff mad, in particular in a meeting-loving culture such as we have today. A meeting audit may be needed. As we spend a large percentage of our time in meetings, they need to be productive. An audit allows all participants to reflect on the process of what works and what doesn't. Ideas to improve on this problem include setting meeting-free periods, encouraging work at home on a personally relevant goal, and deciding who really needs to be in the meeting. A set of ground rules should include the need to stop checking your phone! Some best practices for meetings include, at a minimum, using written meeting agendas with time limits, action items, and follow up. Before scheduling a meeting determine if it's necessary. What are the objectives? Is there an urgency involved? Who needs to be there and what information are they responsible to provide? Scheduling meetings well in advance is important, along with sending out agendas and reading materials, and assuring people show up. Meetings should be short. Does it need to be face-to-face? Meetings that require decisions should allow time for review of the issues and discussion. Each attendee should have a chance to comment on the agenda before launching in. The meeting manager (project manager or facilitator) should provide ground rules for discussion as well as manage the flow of the meeting. Facilitating the group process can be like herding cats. Staying on point is important. The facilitator will need to summarize the conversation and acknowledge points of agreement and contention. Often restating the key points made by the attendees can assist with moving forward. A note taker should be present, even possibly writing decisions on a whiteboard or its virtual equivalent if online.

Changing Business Models

According to Jim Collins, all lasting companies need to reinvent themselves over time. One way museums can do this is to consider developing a program of research and development on new business models. This idea was proposed by Robert Janes in 2009 when he encouraged the field to actively share successes and failures, to develop creativity forums, or to go so far as to create cost-sharing consortia of regional organizations, some of which could be other nonprofits.[15] At a minimum museums should be considering models that serve their customer or audience. In revising operations, revenue models, or collaborations a clear business plan is needed. A business plan is a comprehensive statement of the financial and operational risks and rewards of a proposed enterprise, builds on the strategic plan, and relies heavily on data that prove the feasibility and sustainability of a proposed program. These plans detail the organization's strengths, management, financials, and reputation along with their vision for new ideas. Market analysis is fundamental as is a good risk/reward or return on investment approach. Not enough attention is paid to this phase of planning in the nonprofit sector and museums. But if we are to succeed we need to apply rigorous analysis.

Corporations and Social Value

The corporate world today is aligning itself with values that are similar to nonprofits. Social impact is often a fundamental core value for modern corporations. Consider Starbucks, which works to provide customized and sustainable products and to building competencies in its employees, even providing college degrees. Corporate philanthropy has been a staple of good business practices especially where support to the local community is concerned. Brands are significantly enhanced through doing well. The social mission is also an incentive for recruitment and retention of workers. Wegmans is consistently rated as one of the 100 best companies to work for. A very charitable company, their products are highly rated as well. They pledge continuous improvement to their customers and their people. "We make a difference in every community we serve."[16] They believe in empowering staff. Shared value is a concept gaining momentum. It places emphasis on social impact at the center of the work of the company. Sponsorship of museum programs is an example. Wegmans has worked with educating children for many years by collaborating with museums such as the Strong and the Museum of American History. As corporations become more engaged with this concept they will likely reach out to collaborate with nonprofits in new ways in the future. Or it is possible that they will provide social services that compete with museums.[17]

Stretching the thinking on this concept are new hybrid models. Benefit corporations (B-corps) are an attempt at creating a more efficient system of providing social services. These hybrid organizations are actually for-profit entities that by doing business both make money for investors and deliver a social benefit. Although it is a new concept at least one museum has attempted to use this model. A B-corp was established to form a new gay rights museum in Washington, DC. The CEO Tim Gold stated in an article in 2012: "Being the beneficiary of the Benefit LLC will enable us to attract investors who are not only committed to the museum but who are interested in the bottom line." Certainly the lure of financial sustainability might encourage start-ups to try this format.[18] Another example of alternative financing is the Yerba Buena Arts Center in San Francisco, which is embarking on a collaborative model that draws on financial institutions, community development groups, and others to invest in "social impact artists and their enterprises." The ROI of these investments will be quality of life rather than financial gain.[19]

Sometimes museums determine to do some unique things to sustain themselves financially. In 2015 and again in 2017 the Newseum floated the idea of selling their Pennsylvania Avenue property as a way of avoiding financial disaster. Museums that have fallen victim to accumulating debt after building expansions have notoriously dealt with rescue deals. The Asian Art Museum in San Francisco was saved by the city renegotiating their debt, and the Please Touch Museum in Philadelphia pulled out of bankruptcy through philanthropic support and debt forgiveness. However these are situations to be avoided. A more acceptable approach to new revenue streams may be the practice of providing professional services. The Van Gogh Museum in Amsterdam has created an income stream from international professional consulting. Staff provide services in collections preservation, museum management, and education to individual, corporate, and nonprofit clients. Their practice includes working with Deloitte Luxembourg and the TIAS School for Business and Society.[20]

Collaborations, Partnerships, and Beyond

The proposed Apple Store at Carnegie Library in Washington, DC, is a unique public private partnership that marries the hugely popular retailer with a conservative historical society seeking to transform itself. The historic 1903 building will be renovated to preservation standards and will house both the Apple store and historical society collections, library, and exhibitions. This is an interesting option because Apple has huge financial resources and wishes to turn its stores into experiences featuring concerts, art exhibitions, and photography classes among other programs that mirror the typical museum. This can clearly be seen as "blurring the lines" between for-profit and non-profit and potentially put the historical society at a disadvantage in advancing its traditional content development. But, the museum has suffered from over a decade of turmoil and reinvention. This alliance may be the answer to transforming them into a first class museum facility and forging innovative program ideas.[21]

Another well-tested collaboration is that of three museums in Chattanooga, Tennessee, which decided to form an alliance that served to support their well-being as they opened new riverfront facilities. In 2001 the Hunter Museum of Art, the Tennessee Aquarium, and the Creative Discovery Children's museum determined to go beyond marketing alliances to fundraising and administrative support. The Aquarium with its sophisticated financial, human resources, and technology systems was enlisted to service the needs of the other two museums. But they also have collaborated on exhibitions and completed a joint $120,000,000 capital campaign. While this alliance is a great collaboration, mergers require much more effort, including selecting a single leader and board. In 2006 a merger of Science Place, the Museum of Natural History, and Children's Museum formed the Dallas Museum of Nature and Science. The new entity (rebranded as the Perot Museum of Nature and Science) successfully opened a new facility in 2012. This merger required the blending of the boards, the selection of a new director, and a 10 percent reduction in staff. The project was recognized as a model for nonprofits having received the Lodestar Foundation award in 2009. More of these formal alliances are occurring in the museum field and often they are funded by major gifts of individuals and foundations. It is often the smartest way to create a sustainable organization.[22]

Other innovative partnerships are those meant to advance the diversity of the workforce including collaboration between the Walters Art Gallery and University of Maryland at Baltimore County. Their alliance defines areas of common interest and areas of potential collaboration, such as developing a pipeline for under-served undergraduate and graduate students of color to serve as interns or fellows at the Walters, hosting and cosponsoring exhibitions, and conducting joint research activities.[23]

While all the above collaborations and alliances are attractive and innovative, leaders must be cautious about entering into this new world. Taking time to assess the strengths and weaknesses of the partnership, in particular how each party brings value to the other, is a necessary first step. Will the partner help advance the mission and strategic plan? Joint ventures with for-profits can bring needed expertise and resources. An example would be the projects of the History Channel working with a number of museums to develop films or other experiences for the public. For these relationships to succeed a management plan needs to be developed along with a legal contract for the life of the alliance. Issues of financing, marketing, and brand awareness along with the reputation of the museum need to be considered. A match of values and operating style is important. Business partners will no doubt work at a faster pace than the typical museum. And may be less concerned with the museum's professional standards.[24]

Leading Change in a Digital World

The creation of social change platforms can deepen community engagement, and connect stakeholders in solving critical problems. Beyond a traditional business model, this promises to be a new way of working to advance mission. Anyone with a good idea can build services connecting organizations and citizens in problem solving. One such existing service is the Salesforce.org *Power of Us Hub*—a dynamic platform for resolving social problems.[25] Seeking virtual solutions to social change will be the way of the future. Social change as a platform is first and foremost a business strategy, a theory of change that needs to be integrated into every organization's strategic plan. Common online platforms allow organizations (for-profit or nonprofit) to share information, solutions, and advance problem solving well beyond the internal boundaries of the organization. As to be expected front-runner Nina Simon has applied some of these tools already. Writing in her Museum 2.0 blog she shares how she is moving to avoid bureaucracy at her museum through some new tools such as Slack. This online app allows the staff to share team project information, communicate on a regular basis, and eliminate the use of standard email. "Every channel in Slack is public by default. That means any staff member can check out what's going on in any of our teams or projects." This open form of operations also applies to their office space. Like many firms in Silicon Valley, her staff also work in a common space. Salesforce is used to log data about donors, members, and community partners all of which is available to the museum staff. In addition, all strategic goals are widely tracked and progress is available to all staff.[26]

As we consider the virtual office and a networked world, the ability to influence decision making and change practices should be far easier. Museums have not been shy about building communities of practice around professional best practices over the years. Can we use virtual networks to advance these standards or create new ones? One example might be the group responsible for the manifesto at Active Collections.org. This initiative addresses a problem highlighted by Robert Janes in his book *Museums in a Troubled World*, that of collection building and maintenance over time. This group of largely history museum professionals believes "museums don't just preserve things; they also use them to inspire, enlighten, and connect." And they believe that all collections are not created equal. "We believe some objects support the mission better than others—not based on monetary value or rarity, but based on the stories they tell and the ideas they illuminate. The ones that provide the most public value should get the largest share of our time and resources." The manifesto calls for active sharing, culling, and more thoughtful accessioning. This out of the box thinking is led by professionals who have posted case studies on line suggesting ways to resolve this major issue facing museum leaders today.[27] A similar example is that of Massaction.org generated by staff at the Minneapolis Institute of Art meant to address the following: "How do the museum's internal practices need to change in order to align with, and better inform, their public practice? How can the museum be used as a site for social action? Through a series of public convenings and the creation of a toolkit of resources, this project's intention is to share the strategies and frameworks needed to address these important topics."[28] Ambitious and important goals.

The Transformational Leader

Courageous leaders are needed in a world of constant change and a wide variety of business models, partnerships, and external threats. The qualities that corporations and nonprofits need to look for in creative leaders include:

- An ability to thrive in uncertainty
- Passion to create and own projects
- Skill in persuasion

Although they are more comfortable with risk, they do try to minimize it, much like the profile of innovators described by Adam Grant in *Originals*. These leaders are apt to focus on the development of their ideas and to be more hands on, perhaps standing at the center of the circle than dictating from the top.[29] Who are the transformational leaders in today's museums? Several individuals stand out.

Alex Nyerges, director of the Virginia Museum of Fine Arts, has successfully led his organization through a five-year expansion, strategic planning, and building important exhibition, community education, and outreach programs. Their economic impact in the city and state is substantial and the museum has seen record growth in attendance and membership. The museum is open daily and is free to the public. Their expansion project has allowed the museum to create two high quality restaurants, a new shop, and new spaces for special events and collections. Unlike some directors who are exhausted at the conclusion of a major building project, Nyerges has continued to steward the museum into improved areas of audience engagement.[30] The museum is dedicated to building a diverse workforce, announcing in July 2017 that five women of color hold senior leadership positions.[31]

Another transformational leader is Micah Parzen, CEO of San Diego's Museum of Man. With a PhD in anthropology and a significant law career Parzen brought a set of fresh ideas to the museum in 2010. He promptly dedicated himself to the strategic planning needed to rescue their finances and eventually transform the museum. His focus on team dynamics has been another important accomplishment in transforming the museum's internal culture. Connecting to the community meant picking themes that would resonate such as skateboard culture, race and gender, and immigration. Presenting at the 2016 AAM annual meeting, Parzen spoke of a museum business strategy centered on love and empathy. Seeing the museum as a learning organization he focused on cultural values and brought in consultants on planning and industrial psychology. Attention to staff well-being has been a major focus.[32]

Kaywin Feldman, director and president of the Minneapolis Institute of Art, brings a set of new ideas and innovations to her post. The Institute's 2021 strategic plan builds on many of the external drivers of change, in particular a focus on diversity and inclusion, big data, new technology, and community engagement. Values that underline this plan include stimulating curiosity, building social capital, and delivering personalized experiences. Feldman writes about the need to create a culture that embraces change. "Embracing failure and iterative development are key parts of innovative practice, but this can't just be rhetoric. The journey also includes an examination of institutional culture and challenging traditional assumptions about accepted practice. Museums must develop practiced innovation leaders across the entire institution that can drive experimentation, organizational learning, and strategy refinement." Her efforts focus on creative leaders at all levels and the encouragement of failures as learning tools; and funds are available to seed projects encouraging a culture of research and development.[33] This new organizational transformation is illustrated in a case study presented by staff working with the agile approach in projects. Iterative processes are used to assure continuous improvements, and collaborative staff-wide information sharing and planning. Self-directed work teams are empowered to make decisions. Hearing the common language and testimony of staff is a powerful message that transformation is occurring there.[34]

It's important to acknowledge the work of leaders who have made a long-term impact in the field. Probably one of the most seminal examples is the work of Rollie Adams and his staff at the Strong Museum in Rochester, New York. Beginning in the late 1980s and evolving over several decades, Adams and his staff transformed a traditional history and art museum into an organization dedicated to the topic of play. Over the years the museum created new strategic plans, conducted market research, trained staff in customer service and TQM, established team-based operations, and engaged the community in defining a new model of service to broad audiences. Along the way the museum reinterpreted collections, expanded its facility, and revised their mission to focus on the serious topic of play. As a result the museum today enjoys growing attendance and community support. "The Strong explores play and the ways in which it encourages learning, creativity, and discovery and illuminates cultural history."[35]

Innovative Museum Examples

Museums are taking the lead in becoming centers of innovation. In addition to the lean and agile approach to meeting mission, diversity and inclusion both remain a fundamental anchor driving the change process in museums today. Issues of racial, ethnic, and gender-based diversity have been front and center in museum programming for a number of years. Now efforts are being made to significantly advance the effort to diversify staff. The Field Museum in Chicago, recovering from a number of reorganizations, downsizing, and other disruptions in the past decade, recently launched a workplace culture initiative to better understand the needs of their workforce.[36] Instead of continuing to ignore these issues, smart museum leaders are reaching out to better understand how staff concerns can drive a more productive and relevant organization. Association of Children's Museum executive director Laura Huerta-Migus sees this new emphasis on worker concerns as a way to nurture a positive workplace, assure retention, and reduce turnover, while addressing issues of diversity, a living wage, and benefits.[37]

Other innovations are aimed on public service. Described as the most powerful person in the New York art world, director of the New

Museum in New York City Lisa Phillips has launched incubator programs in art and design. In an interview in the *New York Times* Phillips notes that her leadership style is low key. "The concept of soft power has become a bit of a cliché, I guess. But it's the way I've always thought about what I do, and I think it's the way this museum has made a difference." Her work at the New Museum includes cutting edge exhibitions and "highly experimental programs like an urban think tank and a tech-business incubator, the first of its kind for a museum." The New INC is an incubator space occupied by a variety of tenants. It houses an interdisciplinary community of one hundred members who are investigating new ideas and developing sustainable practices in art, technology, and design.[38]

The list of experimental programs goes on. Freedom's Frontier National Heritage Area in Missouri commemorated the sesquicentennial of Quantrill's Raid on Lawrence, Kansas, through a reenactment on Twitter. The Ohio History Connection opened its Ohio Village to a timeshare arrangement where volunteer interpreters could live in the facilities. Both of these were awarded Leadership in History Awards by the AASLH.[39]

In an era of external threats to core values and in response to the need to support social justice and encourage empathy, museums are talking bold stands. The Levine Museum of the New South in Charlotte, North Carolina, is dedicated to community engagement and providing a forum for issues of social justice. Through exhibitions and public programs they have engaged community on crucial matters facing today's world. The museum espouses a set of core values "that have guided what we do and how we do it: Scholarship, Education, Collaboration, Inclusion, and Fiscal Responsibility." A dialogue on change and diversity has been a primary focus for this museum. After an unfortunate shooting of a citizen in the community and resulting riots the museum took action. Writing about this initiative, CEO Katherine Hill noted, "After the shooting of Keith Lamont Scott, we issued a statement that described Levine's role to help Charlotte understand the present in the context of the past, and importantly, our promise to serve as Charlotte's memory to ensure this moment would not disappear from the community's consciousness with the next news cycle."[40] Other examples include acts of protest in response to political change such as Wellesley College, which draped art works by immigrants in response to the Trump administration ban on immigration. Social media staff in several museums sponsored a #DayofFacts campaign to heighten awareness of attempts to shut down informational websites on science-related data.[41] The above examples are ones that show that museums are dedicated to making an impact. Leaders today need to speak out on social issues and this takes brave and articulate individuals at all levels.

Other examples of supporting the social change effort include sustainable practices. A major issue in many science museums, environmental sustainability takes a major programmatic and operational role. Several museums are taking the lead in applying green practices and providing excellent examples for the public in educational programs and exhibitions. For example, the Phipps Conservatory in Pittsburgh is one of the world's greenest museums. For over twenty years Executive Director Richard Piacentini's passion for sustainability has driven the entire operation from the buildings, to the daily activities, to the dining facility, and to their public programs. Their Center for Sustainable Landscapes is one of eleven buildings in the world that have successfully achieved the Living Building Challenge certification, which is the most rigorous standards-based green building certification. Notes Piacentini, "For us it's about walking the walk and talking the talk. We see a great opportunity for public gardens here and worldwide to provide environmental leadership and inspiration. In order to do that, we look at everything we do—from buildings and gardening practices to food service and operations—and ask, how can we do it better?"[42]

They now have a net zero energy and net zero water facility. Their goal is to get people to think about sustainable behaviors. They recognized that it was very important to connect people to nature, particularly children. From the board down to the front line staff, they live the mission. In fact like many science museums they have divested themselves of fossil fuel stocks to reinvest in renewable energy.[43] Corporate studies note that companies making environmental sustainability a priority have a happier workforce. In these cases staff are trained in best practices, become champions for the cause, and see their ideas about change adopted. This "higher cause" is highly motivating to most employees. It follows that happier workers will be more productive employees and demonstrate dedication to the mission. This is an area that deserves some research to determine whether this premise is true for museums.[44]

The above examples are very much indicative of the contemporary emphasis on *empathy* as espoused by Goleman and other researchers. This value is characteristic of individual leaders who are self-aware, focused, externally observant, and able to filter out the huge number of distractions that face us every day. Stress, discontent, and ambiguity create an atmosphere of anxiety and lead to low morale. Today we see scholarly research and college courses on happiness, a fundamental right often missing in our society. We resolve to be empathetic in our programming, and collaborative in our working relationships. Applying design thinking, adaptive leadership, and agile skills to resolving problems and achieving our mission are tools that make sense in the twenty-first-century museum. A learning organization will constantly be seeking new connections, new solutions, and improving operations. Resisting the hierarchical force field is critical. Shared authority is the challenge for all leaders today. In an era of growing irrelevance, the museum leader needs to take bold steps, to become steward not spectator as Robert Janes has warned us.[45] Writing about this topic, Nina Simon has illustrated best practices that we can take heed of such as her process called "community first" reaching out to various communities through focus groups, volunteers, advisory boards, and in-depth dialogue about what matters.[46]

Reflecting on the lessons of Jim Collins and Jerry Porras in chapter 2, we know that core values are one of the tenets of successful corporations over the long term. Museums today need to focus on their values even more urgently. In the author's experience the world of values has been elusive. As they are defined through the strategic planning process, the museum can easily neglect them in the rush of day to business. But these values are the glue that holds us together as an organization. Subtly they direct our decisions and hit us in the face when we stray from them.

Empathy as a Core Value

Empathy studies show where storytelling, role-playing, and contextualizing history, science, and art with a human connection are vital to visitor learning. As museums become more sophisticated in dealing with empathy, tools are emerging to assist the process. Norris and Tisdale described a process that incorporates emotion in exhibition development. It begins with team learning about the topic and exploring members' own personal responses to varied exhibitions. The conceptual design phase allows for the creation of an "emotional map" illustrating how visitors would experience the objects and layout, incorporating individual voices as a powerful way to share emotion.[47] As a cutting-edge philosophy the dedication to empathy may reside in one area of the organization instead of being embraced by the entire staff and board. A museum-wide dedication to empathy is the ideal model.[48] Innovative museums today are stepping back to reflect on how they deliver social impact, through reexamining mission, management, and finances. Writing about this process Oakland Museum deputy director Kelly McKinley outlined the ultimate goal is to create a social impact statement and related measures of success.[49]

The above examples of modern organizational structures, cross-functional adaptive change systems, transformational leaders, and varied approaches to social impact and empathy are a snapshot of today's innovative leadership. How do we assure that all levels of the organization are capable and comfortable innovators? What of our next generation? We need to discuss how to prepare them for this critical role.

Discussion Questions

1. What practices in your museum are reflective of innovation?
2. How can design thinking be applied to the creation of a new strategic plan?
3. Consider an example of collaboration between museums or museums and for-profits. What are the measures of success in these case studies?
4. What approaches to decision making and rapid prototyping can be implemented at small museums?

Notes

1. Charles Duhigg, *Smarter, Faster, Better* (New York: Random House, 2016), 165.

2. Adam Grant, *Originals, How Nonconformists Move the World* (New York: Viking Press, 2016), 23.

3. Amy C. Edmondson, *Teaming: How Organizations Learn, Innovate, and Compete in the Knowledge Economy* (San Francisco: Jossey-Bass, 2012), 184.

4. Francesco Gino and Bradley Staats, "Why Organizations Don't Learn," *Harvard Business Review* 93, no. 11 (2015): 111–118.

5. Darrell Rigby et al., "Embracing Agile," *Harvard Business Review* 94, no. 5 (May 2016): 40–50.

6. Elizabeth Merritt, "Failing toward Success: The Ascendance of Agile Design," *Museum* 96, no. 2 (2017): 49–52.

7. "Making the Workplace We Want: 4 Lessons from the Getty," March 13, 2017, https://designthinkingformuseums.net/2017/03/13/making-the-workplace-we-want-getty/.

8. Jeanne Liedtka, Andrew King, and Kevin Bennett, *Solving Problems with Design Thinking* (New York: Columbia Business School Publishing, 2013).

9. Dana Mitroff Silvers, "Lean and Smart Human-Centered Design: Three Lessons from the Grand Rapids Art Museum," December 22, 2014, https://designthinkingformuseums.net/2014/12/22/grand-rapids-art-museum/.

10. David Perlman, "New Exploratorium Boss from IDEO Design Firm," *San Francisco Chronicle*, May 12, 2016, http://www.sfgate.com/bayarea/article/New-Exploratorium-boss-from-IDEO-design-firm-7463076.php.

11. Ethan Bernstein, John Bunch, Niko Canner, and Michael Lee, "Beyond the Holacracy Hype," *Harvard Business Review* 94, nos. 7–8 (2016): 39–49.

12. Marty Zwilling, "Build on Demand Teams Instead of Hiring Employees," *Huffington Post*, October 26, 2016, http://www.huffingtonpost.com/marty-zwilling/build-on-demand-teams-ins_b_12651756.html.

13. David A. Garvin, "How Google Sold Its Engineers on Management," *Harvard Business Review*, December 2013, https://hbr.org/2013/12/how-google-sold-its-engineers-on-management.

14. Lecture delivered by Myriam Proulx, business transformation specialist at the Canadian Museum of History, "Changing a National Museum Now for a Sustainable Future," March 3, 2016, George Washington University Museum Studies program class, *Leading Change in Museums*.

15. Robert Janes, *Museums in a Troubled World* (London: Routledge, 2009), 69.

16. See www.wegmans.com.

17. Michael E. Porter and Mark R. Kramer, "Creating Shared Value," *Harvard Business Review* 89, nos. 1–2 (2011): 62–77.

18. Lorraine Mirabella, "Maryland 'B' Corp. Formed to Help Site Search for Proposed Gay Heritage Museum," *Baltimore Sun*, December 7, 2012, http://www.baltimoresun.com/business/bs-bz-gay-museum-bcorp-20121207-story.html.

19. Lecture delivered by Deborah Cullinan, CEO of Yerba Buena Center for the Arts, https://www.museumnext.com/insight/culturebank-new

-investment-paradigm-art-culture/?utm_content=bufferf1dfe&utm_medium
=social&utm_source=twitter.com&utm_campaign=buffer.

20. Nina Siegal, "Van Gogh Museum Wants to Share Its Expertise, for a Price," *New York Times,* May 4, 2016, https://www.nytimes.com/2016/05/04/arts/design/van-gogh-museum-wants-to-share-its-expertise-for-a-price.html.

21. Jonathan O'Connell, "Apple Offers First Peek at Plans to Convert D.C.'s Carnegie Library into a New Store," *Washington Post,* May 8, 2017, https://www.washingtonpost.com/news/digger/wp/2017/05/08/apple-offers-first-peek-at-plans-to-convert-d-c-s-carnegie-library-into-new-store/?utm_term=.2b73864de8e7.

22. Martha Morris, "A More Perfect Union: Museums Merge, Grow Stronger," *Museum* 91, no. 4 (2012): 44–49.

23. Jon Bleiweis, "UMBC and Walters Art Museum Partner to Foster Education, Programs," *Baltimore Sun,* April 12, 2017, http://www.baltimoresun.com/news/maryland/baltimore-county/catonsville/ph-at-umbc-walters-0419-20170412-story.html.

24. James E. Austin and Frances Hesselbein, *Meeting the Collaboration Challenge* (San Francisco: Jossey-Bass, 2002).

25. Barry Libert et al. "How Technology Can Help Solve Societal Problems," *Knowledge at Wharton,* April 21, 2017, http://knowledge.wharton.upenn.edu/article/technology-can-help-solve-societal-problems/.

26. "Growing Bigger Staying Collaborative: 5 Tools for Building Non-Bureaucratic Organizations," December 19, 2016, http://museumtwo.blogspot.com/2016/12/growing-bigger-staying-collaborative-5.html?platform=hootsuite.

27. Manifesto at ActiveCollections.org, http://www.activecollections.org.

28. See https://www.museumaction.org.

29. Timothy Butler, "Hiring an Entrepreneurial Leader," *Harvard Business Review* 95, no. 2 (2017): 85–93.

30. Katherine Calos, "Five Years after Expansion, VMFA Impact Soars," *Richmond Times-Dispatch,* August 31, 2015, http://www.richmond.com/news/local/city-of-richmond/five-years-after-expansion-vmfa-impact-soars/article_6ff46ace-1a42-5d9f-a6cc-cf556068b5a9.html.

31. Holly Rodriguez, "Five African American Women Hold Senior Leadership Positions," *Richmond Free Press,* July 14, 2017, http://richmondfreepress.com/news/2017/jul/14/5-african-american-women-hold-senior-leadership-po/.

32. Micah Parzen, "What's Love Got to Do with It," panel presentation at the American Alliance of Museums annual meeting, May 2016; and Marsha

Semmel "Museum Leadership, Organizational Readiness, and Institutional Transformation," *Museum* 96, no. 2 (2017): 21–26.

33. Kaywin Feldman, "Creating Your Team, A Talent Strategy for Innovation," blog post, http://www.museum-id.com/idea-detail.asp?id=520#.

34. Douglas Hegley, Meaghan Tongen, and Andrew David, "The Agile Museum," paper presented at Museums and the Web Conference, 2016, http://mw2016.museumsandtheweb.com/paper/the-agile-museum/.

35. Amy Hollister Zarlengo, "The Great Transformation at the Strong," in *Case Studies in Cultural Entrepreneurship*, ed. Gretchen Sorin and Lynne Sessions (Lanham, MD: Rowman & Littlefield, 2015), 65–87.

36. American Alliance of Museums Labs Blog, http://labs.aam-us.org/blog/workplace-culture-lets-talk-about-it/.

37. Author conversation with Laura Huerta-Migus, June 8, 2017.

38. Randy Kennedy, "The Most Powerful Woman in the New York Art World," *New York Times,* May 5, 2017, https://www.nytimes.com/2017/05/04/arts/design/new-museum-director-lisa-phillips.html?_r=0.

39. AASLH, "Audience Engagement Techniques from Award Winners," blog post, http://blogs.aaslh.org/creative-audience-engagement-techniques-from-award-winners/.

40. Kathryn Hill, "Knowing Justice and Peace in Times of Crisis," blog post, http://futureofmuseums.blogspot.com/2016/10/knowing-justice-and-peace-in-times-of.html?m=1.

41. Graham Bowley, "Museums Chart a Response to Political Upheaval," *New York Times,* March 13, 2017, https://www.nytimes.com/2017/03/13/arts/design/museums-politics-protest-j20-art-strike.html.

42. "Zoom In: Richard V. Piacentini," April 2017, http://www.meetingstoday.com/Article-Details/ArticleID/30200.

43. Richard Piacentini, "Lessons Learned: Museum Building Projects," paper presented at the American Alliance of Museums Annual Meeting, May 27, 2016.

44. C. B. Bhattacharya, "How Companies Can Tap Sustainability to Motivate Staff," *Knowledge at Wharton,* September 29, 2016, http://knowledge.wharton.upenn.edu/article/how-companies-tap-sustainability-to-motivate-staff/?utm_source=kw_newsletter&utm_medium=email&utm_campaign=2016-09-29.

45. Janes, *Museums in a Troubled World,* 169.

46. Nina Simon, *The Art of Relevance* (Santa Cruz, CA: Museum 2.0, 2016), 99.

47. Linda Norris and Rainey Tisdale, "Developing a Toolkit for Emotion in Museums," *Exhibitionist* 36, no. 1 (2017): 100–108.

48. See the blog post by Director of Education & Public Programs at Portland Art Museum, Mike Murawski, calling for more widespread adoption of empathy, https://artmuseumteaching.com/2016/07/11/the-urgency -of-empathy-social-impact-in-museums/.

49. Kelly McKinley, "What Is Our Museum's Social Impact?" July 10, 2017, https://medium.com/new-faces-new-spaces/what-is-our-museums-social -impact-62525fe88d16.

LEADERSHIP DEVELOPMENT

THE NEXT GENERATION

The future of museum work presents many obstacles and opportunities. As discussed in chapter 1 the rise of a flexible workforce and the desire of emerging professionals for multiple job opportunities over their careers require a new mind-set. As technology evolves leaders will need to deal with the reality of a virtual work environment. Even more complex is the potential of artificial intelligence and robotics replacing traditional work and altering our communications systems. As trends predict, leaders in the future need to be strong on emotional intelligence, cross-cultural dexterity, and creative problem solving. Museums need tech savvy, globally astute workers with a sense of audience needs. And in many cases both financial acumen and major building projects experience will be mandatory.[1]

The leadership challenge is even more urgent today than in the past as we see a generation of seasoned individuals leaving the workforce. In the arts in particular filling vacant positions will continue to be the norm. Art museum directorships are in constant flux. In 2015 the city of Boston saw three top positions change hands—at the Museum of Fine Arts, Harvard Art Museums, and the Isabelle Stewart Gardner Museum. Close to one-third of all art museum directors are reaching retirement age, creating a crisis for boards looking for the best talent.[2] Not just directors will be leaving, but individuals in many key museum jobs including curators, registrars, educators, and conservators. Hopefully, this transition will provide an opportunity for younger and more diverse candidates to rise up. Another issue to address is multiple generations in the workforce. In 2016 the William and Flora Hewlett Foundation announced a new focus on training multi-generational workers. Despite the pending exodus of Baby Boomers, some older workers in later stages of their careers are not retiring due to economic and other personal factors.[3] Fortunately, at the 2017 AAM annual meeting this very issue was discussed by an intergenerational panel. Insights were shared that pointed to a need to work on problem solving not only across the functions in museums, but also with generational diversity in mind. This approach draws on the strengths and deep knowledge of seasoned staff members as well as the skill and passion of younger employees.[4]

What Skills Are Needed Now?

It is important to take a closer look at what museum decision makers are seeking in leaders today. How do boards describe the skills needed in their top leadership posts? It is not one size fits all. Skills and abilities vary depending on the type and size of museum, as well as its place on the organizational life cycle. Two examples of recruitments in 2017 reflect this divergence. The Elmhurst (Illinois) History Museum director reports to the city manager, not a board of trustees. The job includes collecting, exhibitions, and educational programs while collaborating with a fundraising foundation and the city government. Four years of experience is required including computer literacy and fundraising software experience. On a different scale is the president and CEO of the Historic Charleston (South Carolina) Foundation. This position requires collaboration, strategic thinking, interpersonal skill, change management, visionary leadership, and fifteen years' experience. The Elmhurst Museum has a budget of under 500,000 dollars with visitation of 15,000 per year while the Charleston Foundation has a budget of 5,000,000 dollars with a mission to preserve and interpret several historic structures in the city.[5] Clearly the size of the community, the governance structure, the size and number of facilities and staff as well as visitation and programs are among the criteria for defining the profile of the leader. A museum that needs to reengage with its community or with a younger generation may seek a leader with a track record in education, technology, or marketing and social media. When the Metropolitan Museum announced the resignation of Thomas P. Campbell as Director and the promotion of Daniel Weiss to president and CEO in the summer of 2017, many questions arose about the process of executive succession as well as the definition of their roles and responsibilities. Facing financial troubles the museum needed a leader with business skills. In an organization that has long relied on dual leadership (artistic and administrative) it is clear that perils await when well-defined plans and policies are missing. Not a new model, it still brings with it considerable ambiguity and inherent power struggles.[6]

What Do Surveys Reveal?

Several studies of museum leaders and staff point to a variety of skills needed to succeed in the museum workforce. Examining what hiring officials are looking for at the entry level is a good start. A study conducted by William Bomar, executive director of the University of Alabama Museums, published in 2013 highlighted the following desirable skills as mentioned by museum leaders:

- Communications (oral and written)
- Community engagement
- Financial management
- Interpersonal relations
- Project management
- Technology

These skills were emphasized over the obvious professional and programmatic expertise expected of most museum staff. How these skills will be obtained is the next question. In some cases they are taught in museum studies programs, but for the most part entry-level individuals may be on their own to get the needed training.[7] A survey of sixteen museum directors conducted by the author in 2012 revealed a set of skills that museum leaders need to assure success, including

- Board development
- Change management
- Fundraising
- Leadership skill
- Strategic planning

These directors described a successful leader as one with vision, an entrepreneurial mind-set, facilitation skill, and ability to manage large-scale projects. Also mentioned were financial literacy, team-building, project management, negotiation, marketing, and ethics. A parallel survey asked similar questions of mid-career museum staff. The feedback from the 159 respondents revealed a need for the following skills:

- Change management
- Financial acumen
- Project management
- Teamwork
- Strategic planning

All of the above surveys clearly cover many of the same concerns for building strong leaders in the museum workplace. In the mid-career survey time management was also mentioned as a challenge, a great indicator of a stressed workforce. Other thoughts and concerns raised by these individuals revealed that their senior managers did not have adequate leadership skills. And, for those who had taken some training, many expressed frustration at being unable to implement new ideas and approaches back in the workplace, including the reality of peer resentment.[8] Looking abroad, a comprehensive survey of museum professionals in Great Britain revealed emphasis on diversity, digital skills, collaboration, innovation, and financial resilience. In addition, respondents felt their organizations were lacking in fair pay, managing change, and professional development.[9]

In summary, many of these issues raise the deep-seated need for leadership training at all levels. Some of the needs are rather fundamental; and the field needs to craft programs that will deal with more complex issues including volatility, climate change, economic inequality, competition for positions, fair pay, and funding crises. Aside from a deep understanding of the standards and best practices of the field, museum workers seeking leadership roles will need strategic thinking, self-awareness, collaboration, and understanding of credible metrics as a basis of decision making.[10] And, obviously a strong emphasis on financial skills, fundraising, and board relations are fundamentals in preparing for taking on the top job in museums today.

Museums as a Learning Environment

Fundamental to skill building is the need to learn on the job and from peers as opposed to formal educational training. Action Learning involves applying varied approaches to problem solving and learning through an iterative process. This is often the best way to gain skill and self-confidence for museum professionals. Museums that spend time and money on developing their staff find that empowerment is the biggest motivator. In a survey conducted by the author in 1995, museum respondents noted that leaders needed to focus on big picture strategy while staff needed to serve as internal advisors to management to assure best practices for improving operations. These individuals were empowered to make decisions that impact the visitor experience without checking with senior staff.[11]

What are museums doing today to encourage a learning environment? There are a number of excellent examples. Kentucky Science Center's CEO Jo Haas is a passionate believer in supporting the development of new leaders at all levels at her museum. She works to "foster an environment that expects excellence, encourages experimentation, and allows for failure." And much as she did as a rising leader, she constantly gives short-term projects to staff as a learning experience.[12] For example nonprogram staff were selected to create educational programs at her museum. The teams were given seed money and a timeline to create interactive experiences. Staff who were involved immediately learned something new about the operations of other departments, and increased respect for each other's roles.[13] Haas currently conducts monthly brown bag lunch sessions with her "next generation leadership team" encouraging open dialogue on a variety of topics.[14]

Aside from the opportunities afforded by enlightened leaders, staff members should seek out their own path to the top. Taking the leap to learn about the organization and make a difference is one step. An example is that of Lori Fogarty CEO of the Oakland Museum who advised "I think you have to look for opportunities to play a leadership role, at any level. I'm a huge believer that there are people within the middle management level of every organization that really make a difference. And they usually show a great attitude."[15]

The importance of self-renewal is often overlooked. In 1990 Peter Drucker advocated for a process that encourages a leader to become a teacher, to serve another organization, and serve "down in the ranks."[16] The advice is still pertinent today. Teaching others about your work allows you to reflect on what really matters while at the same time seeking feedback. Service to other organizations such as volunteering or sitting on a board gives perspective, and serving in the ranks is perhaps the most important. For those who hold senior positions, the "undercover boss" approach of working alongside staff at various levels of the organization brings amazing new insights.

Taking a closer look at the next generation of leadership reveals more about the expectations of emerging professionals. A study by SAP predicts that 50 percent of the workforce in 2020 will be millennials. Of these 91 percent aspire to be in leadership. They also have critical views on the leadership skills and styles needed today. The qualities mentioned in the SAP study reflect the thinking of many emerging museum professionals as well, including

- a social impact mission
- a digitally savvy environment
- an inclusive and transparent management
- an emphasis on diversity
- staff development opportunities
- work life balance and flexibility

In regard to the development of millennials in the workforce, "The corporate ladder is gone. The corporate lattice is here. The lattice career creates career paths that move laterally, diagonally, and down, as well as up." The role of mentors is central to this new approach.[17] An example of the lattice approach is the case study of Nathan Ritchie writing in *Museum* magazine. His career progressed from high school to the National Park Service, to graduate school in San Francisco, to a small art museum in Indiana, to a start-up in Chicago, to the position of director of the Golden History museum in Colorado. Ritchie is an educator by training. This willingness to move from one location to another over a relatively short period of time finally landed him at his dream job.[18]

The Leadership Continuum

Leadership skill is something that develops over one's career. The IMLS in collaboration with the Educopia Institute and Center for Creative Leadership developed the *Layers of Leadership* framework to outline skills and roles needed for various aspects of leadership development. The following are descriptive layers including

- Self
- Others
- Departments
- Organizational
- Field-wide

For each layer a set of tasks, skills, and outcomes are defined. For example in Layer 2—Leading Others—*tasks* include empowering staff, inspiring creativity, teambuilding, and public speaking while *skills* include conflict resolution, agile learning, boundary spanning, and recognizing talent. The outcome should be productivity at the collaborative team level. At each of the five levels the skills are more complex and impactful. The end goal of this framework is yet another opportunity for individual leadership development. Of course, not every career will require all of these layers, but the document can serve as a guide for individual professional development. Just as we see a life cycle for organizational growth, this layered framework could serve to mirror the professional development timeline.[19]

Mentorships and Leadership Development

The workplace is the training ground for many museum staff, and mentors are often of incredible influence in the process. Whether a formal match with a senior staff member or a link to members of professional interest groups or even someone outside the field, a mentor can add immeasurably to the self-assessment process. Former art museum director Michael Shapiro has placed a spotlight on the mentorship process. In his own experience and that of eleven museum directors he interviewed careers bloomed from working with teachers, colleagues, supervisors, and others. Thelma Golden, director and chief curator at the Studio Museum of Harlem, notes "Whom you work for has an incredible amount to do with your career and how it might progress." Her growth was the result of interaction with artists, curators, and directors who served as inspiration and mentored her to be her best.[20] Directors featured in Shapiro's text provided valuable insights and advice including the need to hold back on the race to the corner office, to know your staff including the guards, and to say thank you consistently.

The value of mentorships goes both ways. Often the mentee has insights that can be helpful to their mentor. Successful mentorships involve coaching, commiseration, and problem solving. Mentors can also serve to sponsor an emerging professional as they move up the ladder or along the lattice. This underscores the value of the intergenerational learning mentioned above. When we think about the enormous turnover in seasoned museum professionals facing the field it is a no-brainer that these people can be a major resource to the next generation. Providing the older worker part-time employment and the ability to serve as mentors and thought leaders in the field is a positive. This approach has been implemented at several Smithsonian museums in recent years.

Aside from the role of mentors, it goes without saying that supervisors must play a critical role in developing their staff. One area that remains consistently controversial is that of the formal appraisal. Performance evaluations are losing popularity yet there are ways to use this system to strengthen learning organization goals. What seems to be happening is a morphing of the process over time. Instead of the traditional approach of developing goals and measuring outcomes on an annual basis, more frequent communications with employees is needed. New team-based and agile work models do not focus on reflecting on past accomplishments, but look to what needs to be done to improve current, iterative work goals. Thus, a focus on learning is more important than measuring accountability. More modern systems are trying the 360-degree assessment that is important to team success.

Other ways that the individual in the organization can learn from agile approaches might be in adopting some corporate practices. As discussed in chapter 6, the social value of corporations is leading to new practices. Microsoft has launched annual hackathons to address social issues through self-selected teams that develop new business models for resolving critical problems in communities. Corporations also invest in high risk projects that focus on outcomes that may lead to failures (as in rapid prototyping and design thinking), yet encourage staff to be part of the thought leader process in the company.[21] Forward thinking museums will need to consider adopting these options as ways to strengthen staff skills and flexibility.

What Can Individual Workers Do?

The reality of becoming a leader is very much a personal journey. While museums can and should provide opportunities for their staff members, the growth necessary is really up to the individual. A trait frequently mentioned as a sign of a modern leader is self-awareness. The issue can be complex in that self-awareness is not only knowing yourself and your learning style and goals, but knowing what others think of you as a leader. Studies have found that leaders often fail in the latter category and making the leap to this second dimension of self-awareness takes effort. Self-awareness also means that a leader understands the power dynamic of their role. It is important to realize that once in a leadership role your relationship with colleagues and subordinates will change. Being sensitive to the reality can assure that you don't take yourself too seriously! Self-awareness is closely aligned with compassion. Not only for others but oneself. In fact, reflecting on one's strengths and the people and organizations that have contributed to personal growth are grounds for a happier individual.

On a practical note, there are several steps that a museum staff member should take to assure they are considered for career progression in the workplace. Individuals need to understand the organizational structure and strategic direction of the museum. They need to make an effort to meet board members and invite them and the director to learn more about their work in the museum. Further, being a part of the process of developing, implementing, and assessing suc-cess of strategic plans is crucial. Embracing the team approach and being brave enough to speak up in support of important policies or decisions helps to advance an individual's stature and standing in the museum. All staff should understand the budget and what role they play in assuring funds are spent wisely. Writing in *A Life in Museums: Managing Your Museum Career*, Wendy Blackwell speaks candidly of lessons to be learned in the workplace including observing corpo-rate culture, working with different generations, being supportive of the goals of your supervisor, and being counted on to get the work done.[22] Blackwell speaks of her experience working in a completely different field, as a railroad station manager. Building on the lessons of that work her career progressed to museum education and eventually director of the National Children's Museum.

Learning to be a new leader or simply a better leader is critical and something pursued by many museum workers. There are a number of options. Degree programs, short courses, workshops, mentorships, internal rotation and staff development programs, skill exchanges with other museums, and executive coaching are all options. Being informed about leadership trends, skills, and expectations of hiring boards or other officials takes a lot of effort. Aside from the publica-tions related to museums and the arts, periodicals such as *Harvard Business Review, Inc., Fast Company, Forbes, Chronicle of Philanthropy, Nonprofit Quarterly,* and *Wired* can all provide interesting perspec-tives on leadership trends. Other readings are those related to psy-chology, organizational science, and human resource management. Lifelong learning allows individuals to expand their creativity and add significantly to the success of the organization; so reading outside your field should be mandatory. Divergent thinking and experimenta-tion can add to your creative practice. Should an individual have their sights on a top-level CEO position, a search firm may be the first level of communication. Understanding how these firms operate will help position a candidate in the best light. Executive recruiters have good information on their websites and consulting with others who have been through the process can be of value.

Leadership training programs abound in the corporate and non-profit sectors. This is big business in itself. But how do they measure up? In many cases these programs are less than satisfactory. Despite sophisticated training programs that immerse workers in best practices, there are barriers to implementing these newly acquired skills. First, taking these skills back to the workplace is dicey. For most organizations, entrenched modes of operating will resist any new approaches. The excitement of fresh ideas learned at a leadership training workshop or even a new degree will be up against the status quo of the workplace. Often the employee slips back into the pre-training mode. Resolving this problem requires a new way of thinking throughout the organization starting at the top. Education and training will succeed in organizations that have a mandate for change and that encourage implementation of newly acquired practices. So, in the long term it is incumbent upon senior management to fix broken systems and policies. Since this links closely to the change process these areas need attention.[23]

Museum Leadership Training Options

The museum field has many options for training in leadership skills including advanced degrees. Today the MBA maybe a dream for many as the cost can be prohibitive. Anyone with existing student loans will certainly think twice about taking on the enormous expense of the MBA. Fortunately, there are many options for workshops, webinars, and other forms of continuing education. Some of these are designed and offered by individual museums while others are meant to provide skills training for a cohort composed of professionals from varied museums. Most have a goal of creating a network of future colleagues as well as helping a future leader feel more confident in dealing with the board and other influential individuals such as donors. The Getty Leadership Institute at Claremont College in California has been training senior managers for several decades. Other programs include the Center for Curatorial Leadership at Columbia University (training art museum curators for ascension to the director's chair), the 21st Century Leadership Skills Seminar at George Washington University with the Smithsonian, and Cooperstown's Institute for Cultural Entrepreneurship. Museum associations also offer their own training such as the Jekyll Island Management Institute sponsored by the Southeast Museum Conference and Developing History Leaders sponsored by AASLH. Each of these programs offers updated thinking on leadership trends and prepares the individual for implementing new ideas at their home museum.

Museums that provide their own training include the Metropolitan Museum and Smithsonian Institution. The latter has established the Palmer Leadership Program for mid-level and senior managers at the Smithsonian. Cohorts of up to twenty-five individuals are assigned mentors and spend one year in rotations, readings, lectures, and team projects. The Clore Leadership program in Great Britain has trained twenty to thirty individuals per year since 2004 and offers workshops and residential courses, an extended museum placement, individually selected training, mentoring, and coaching. The success of the program has been extended to include emerging museum professionals, two-day follow up courses, extension to international markets, and board development.[24] This program is close in scope to the Getty training programs. Getty has developed programs for international cohorts, for emerging professionals, and for individuals in senior positions. The format includes both online and in person training. Often the individuals are taught by business school faculty and current museum leaders. Team projects are emphasized, along with self-assessments, and ideas for implementing change at their home museums.

Not all training is focused on modern business practices. Today we see some unusual position titles such as chief content officer, chief wonder officer, or museum hacktivist! Beyond traditional training options, there are programs such as that launched by the Denver Museum of Contemporary Art. With funding from the Mellon Foundation the museum created a series of innovation fellowships around the mission of sharing best practices throughout the country. The goal is to reinvigorate museum programming and increase attendance. This involves a 10-day residency workshop, ongoing mentorship, and a final group project. This is a program meant to groom the next generation of museum creatives.[25]

Does Museum Leadership Training Make a Difference?

As noted above challenges exist in assuring that lessons learned in training programs stick. How do we assure that the new skills developed in a workshop, or degree program will actually make a difference in the workplace and in the career development of the individual? Insight from attendees of various leadership training programs is helpful. Lauren Telchin-Katz, a senior project manager at the National Museum of American History, participated in the Smithsonian's Palmer program in 2016. Her experience was a positive one. She reports an increased level of confidence especially in managing up. Over the course of a year her cohort met on a regular basis, completed team projects, read business literature, and interacted with managers around the Smithsonian. The program provides a 360-degree assessment where participants receive feedback from supervisors, colleagues, and direct reports. Each participant meets with their director and is assigned a buddy and a senior staff mentor. Part of the training includes crucial conversations and learning about the institutional budget process. Networking is an important part of the process. Her team project was to study the exhibition development process at a variety of museums with the goal to improve systems at the museum.[26]

Another individual who has taken advantage of mid-career training programs is Allison Titman, accreditation program officer at the American Alliance of Museums. Titman participated in the 21st Century Leadership Skills Seminar at GWU. As a result, she was inspired to continue her professional leadership training via the eight-month certificate program offered by National Arts Strategies and the School of Social Policy and Practice at the University of Pennsylvania. This immersive course work afforded Titman continued skills development in business planning, budgets, the creation of logic models, and thinking about personal leadership style. As a result she can now easily read a financial audit, speak up more confidently at work, and negotiate for important initiatives. This inspired her to seek an online MBA from the University of Maryland. The value of these training opportunities is their flexibility, allowing her to grow at her own pace.[27]

As Peter Drucker has advised, smart leaders consistently seek opportunities to renew themselves. Working with a cohort of other like-minded and passionate professionals in a new setting can be reinvigorating and enlightening. This is one of the values of a convening such as the 21st Century Leadership Skills Seminar. Jessica Nicoll, a seasoned museum director currently running the Smith College Museum of Art, reflected on her experience in the seminar. She notes

"The leadership seminar was timely and valuable for me. It fell at the midpoint in our strategic planning process, as we were just digesting research and starting to identify priorities. One of the outcomes of a workshopping session in the seminar challenged me to consider whether our evolving vision was ambitious enough in promoting positive institutional change (and not just sustaining established success). I took that to heart and, . . . dove back into our planning process and pushed to think bigger and more ambitiously." This resulted in significant grant funding to enable the initiatives in the plan. Nicoll also was inspired to create more protected time in her schedule for collecting her thoughts as she worked toward the implementation of the plan. She also was challenged by a major institutional change with a wave of retirements. Working closely with her staff in a time of change was mandatory and she was able to draw on "coaching and skills developed in the program, particularly around managing challenging conversations."[28]

Clearly taking charge of one's leadership development is the critical strategy. Despite the rising number of training workshops, degrees, and formal mentorship programs in nonprofit and museum leadership, the bottom line is that individuals must seek the best opportunities for growth. Listening, observing, and learning are critical. Seek mentors, take on unpopular or risky projects, polish communications skills, and help other people shine. And work on your sense of humor and humility. Networking will advance one's ability to learn and move toward success. Many successful senior leaders seek each other out in formal and informal discussion groups either at conferences or in their communities. They never stop learning and problem solving.

Diversity, Inclusion, and Equity as a Mandate

Museums today need to be part of the solution not the problem of diversity in the workforce. Recent surveys have shown a startling lack of diversity in museum staffing including CEO positions and the board level. Surveys published in 2015 revealed that 72 percent of the museum workforce is white and 60 percent female; and therein lies a fundamental weakness.[29] As a result the field is redoubling its effort to shine a spotlight on this issue. Foundations are assisting in the process, as are prominent museum leaders. For example, Rod Bigelow of Crystal Bridges Museum of American Art in Arkansas, revised his title to executive director and chief diversity and inclusion officer. Others are following this lead and setting targets to provide a more inclusive workforce. The Speed Art Museum in Louisville developed a new board metric that includes categories such as race, age, gender, profession, financial capacity, and creative thinking.[30]

Even in those museums which have committed to diversity in programs, collections, and staffing there can be barriers to opportunities for professional advancement of the diverse workforce. Looking at the challenges of leadership opportunities for women today, Anne Ackerson and Joan Baldwin surveyed over 500 women in the field regarding their expectations and experiences. Several concerns were raised by these individuals, including[31]

- Pay inequity and sexism
- Professional advancement barriers
- Work-life balance
- Risk averse boards and senior managers
- Lack of self-confidence

Following on this research is the reality of gender bias in the workplace. A study of women's success in reaching CEO status in the corporate world found only 6 percent of Fortune 500 companies have female CEOs. More deeply rooted barriers exist and mental models see women as dependable, uncompetitive, and not visionary. Often women who work assertively find resistance from male and female colleagues. Clearly this is a problem when a large percentage of the museum workforce is female.[32]

However, diversity and inclusion must be addressed if museums are to survive and thrive. Millennial generations are taking this to heart. Museum associations are moving forward with this as a key strategy as are many individual museums. Just as collections preservation, community engagement, and sound management practices have been supported by the field, a new generation is focused on issues of equity. Forward thinking museums are implementing policies and practices that seek diversity at all levels. The conscious effort plays out with strategies to attract diverse candidate pools for interns, fellows, and permanent staff. For example, museums are concentrating on high school programs for volunteers, teen-led workshops and tours, and behind the scenes work with existing staff. The AAM has hired a diversity and inclusion officer. Other museums have established cultural competency training and sought to work on barriers. In a lecture at George Washington University, Laura Huerta Migus, executive director of the Association of Children's Museums, highlighted that barriers exist within the museum itself as the traditional routes to leadership positions are mainly biased to those individuals with advanced degrees (e.g., curators). As there are few managerial jobs in the field, and low turnover in those ranks, there is paucity of opportunity. Huerta-Migus notes that, based on recent workforce surveys, those people in administrative roles (events, marketing, finance, or facilities) are more diverse with respect to race, ethnicity, and gender. Frontline staff also are at a disadvantage due to temporary or part-time status and not given opportunities to advance.[33]

Recognizing the importance of these issues in the field, the Museum Studies Program at GWU hosted a 2017 convention around the topic of diversity and inclusion attended by university educators, museum professionals, grant makers, AAM staff, museum workers, and students of color. Many excellent ideas were advanced including the need to establish pipelines in public schools and local communities; provide cultural competency training for museum staff; to increase emphasis on staff development; and to make this a requirement for AAM accreditation. Building a community of activists is a way forward. Mentorships are needed as well as financial incentives to provide paid internships and professional training. Students today do not see museum work as rewarding, nor do they see themselves working in museums. Low wages continue to be a barrier. For those in the workforce, skills such as communications and financial savvy are needed.

Museum leaders today are advancing the cause. A case study of a forward-thinking executive director is that of Marilee Jennings, of the Children's Discovery Museum of San Jose. Her initiative in developing a more diverse workforce includes many activities including offering competitive salaries, assigning internal mentors, and hiring strategically to reflect the demographics of her community. The impetus for the diversity initiative came after a drop in museum attendance. Looking more closely at this decline, Jennings saw a need to attract the more diverse members of the community, especially the Latino population.

Seeking input from community leaders was a first step, particularly those from the media. The Latino population has been growing five times faster than any other ethnicity and they have a 200-year history in the region. Jennings learned that their messages to this community were not welcoming. So steps were taken to add dual language publications, an exhibition from Mexico City, and a traditional Dia de los Tres Reyes Magos festival during the Christmas holiday season.

Beyond this new programming, they focused on diversifying the "audience facing staff" through attending high school and junior college job fairs, and advertising positions in Spanish language publications. They found that the younger generations were attracted to jobs at the museum as they tend to enjoy working with young children. A strategic hire was a floor supervisor from the Mexican community who effectively recruited young Latinos to their first jobs. Jennings noted that the media was a critical factor in getting the word out including social media. Recognizing the need to prepare new staff members for a career progression was the next challenge. As mid-level jobs opened at the museum Jennings was sure to fill them with internal candidates of color. She has also provided more skill building through a program of online workshops aimed at training staff.[34]

In 2017 the city of New York announced that they would tie funding for their arts and cultural agencies to their emphasis on an inclusive workforce. This new policy initiative is hopeful but represents a shift away from funding based solely on mission or numbers of community members served. Instead the city will now look for progress in diversifying the workforce as the basis for receiving funds.[35]

How do we assure that internal structures are in place to support a more diverse workforce? The progress of many organizations is slowed down due to internal resistance and biases. Studies show that standard corporate programs requiring mandatory training in diversity do not succeed in changing the makeup of the workforce. This is due to the fact that mandatory training and grievance systems often emphasize legal cases and other penalties. Managers often feel anger and resistance. The study went on to discuss positive steps that organizations have taken to resolve this problem. They include making training voluntary, cross training among difference sections of the company, recruitment of women and minorities at college fairs, assigning mentors to diverse staff members, and establishing task forces to tackle issues of "social accountability." Underlying the success of these programs is increased contact among diverse groups in the workplace.[36] In fact unconscious gender bias is a real issue in all organizations. Yet in the view of a hiring manager diversity should be seen as a strength. In the twenty-first-century organization, we know that diversity of ideas and viewpoints will lead to more vibrant and relevant ideas for achieving mission. In hiring it is not unusual to look for people like ourselves (with the requisite liberal arts degrees and museum training), but to allow for diversity we need to look beyond this. Hiring community organizers, marketing and social media specialists, or practicing artists for key jobs can bring new talents and perspectives to the task at hand. In addition there are options to hire executive search firms that specialize in diversity or even nonprofit consultants such as Race Forward working with several arts organizations in New York City on strategies for diversifying staff.[37]

Paying attention to salary is another factor. In response to the concerns raised by Museum Workers Speak, paid internships must become a common practice. Fair pay for all workers needs to be a priority. Closely linked to the issue of equal rights and fair treatment is the reality of a living wage. The findings of the 2017 Association of Art Museum Directors (AAMD) salary survey validated the reality that senior levels of the art museum field make far higher salaries than the rank and file. Trends saw an increase in salary levels for directors, chief operating officers, and technology staff. And at the same time the gender gap remains an issue with women museum directors making less than their male counterparts. Senior level museum staff are averaging in the six-figure range, while lower level staff average around $50,000.[38] Even where efforts are being made to raise salaries for museum workers a Catch 22 exists. In Great Britain where a National Living Wage mandate raised salaries for museum workers, museums were found to practice belt tightening, use volunteer or contract labor, and increase admission fees. This low pay dilemma has been for years the "price people pay for doing a job they love."[39] And as wages are depressed, fewer individuals of color will be drawn to the field. The seriousness of the situation has led to the formal intervention of unions to represent workers in both Great Britain and the United States. It is likely that this type of action will be an important option for museum workers into the future, particularly with the power of networking and crowd advocacy in the creation of social change platforms as mentioned in chapter 6. The fact is that millennials are more than ready to take up the charge in highlighting the issue of contract employment and unpaid internships as potential unfair labor practices. Museum Workers Speak and their future iterations need to take this on. Museums save money by contracting and these individuals have no benefits and no rights.

Looking back over the challenges and opportunities of preparing leaders, it is clear that ethically our workforce deserves much more support and opportunity. A three-legged stool approach includes a network of professionals pressuring for positive change, individual museum leaders, and board members modeling the best practices for preparing their staff, and workers themselves taking responsibility for self-development and fair treatment.

Discussion Questions

1. What skills do you think will make a difference in sustaining your museum in the next decade?
2. Is there a staff development or mentorship program in place at your museum? How do you participate?
3. Should museum directors have business training to be effective?
4. How can diversity and inclusion practices be activated in your professional networks?

Notes

1. Karie Willyerd and Barbara Mistick, *Stretch: How to Future-Proof Yourself for Tomorrow's Workplace* (Hoboken, NJ: John Wiley, 2016), 187–203.

2. "Onward and Upward," *Economist*, May 9, 2015, https://www.economist .com/news/books-and-arts/21650523-more-third-american-art-museum -directors-are-retirement-age-those-charge.

3. John E. McGirk, "What Do Arts Leaders Really Need," blog post, March 10, 2016, http://www.hewlett.org/what-do-arts-leaders-really-need/.

4. Marsha L. Semmel, Elizabeth Isele, Samuel Moore, and Greg Stevens, "Generational Inclusion: Shattering Stereotypes and Challenging Assumptions," *Informal Learning Review* (ILR) no. 144 (May/June 2017). A copyrighted publication of Informal Learning Experiences, Inc.

5. Information from job announcements posted on the AASLH job-seeker website on July 18, 2017, http://careerwebsite.com/jobseeker/search/results/?str=1&site_id=22344&max=25&sort=start_&vnet=0&long=1.

6. Robin Pogrebin, "Met Museum Changes Leadership Structure," *New York Times,* June 13, 2017, https://www.nytimes.com/2017/06/13/arts/design/met-museum-changes-leadership-structure.html.

7. William F. Bomar, "Skills Most Valued for Entry-Level Professional Museum Positions," *AASLH Technical Leaflet 261,* 2013.

8. The findings were the results of a survey of museum leaders and workers regarding leadership skills training, conducted by the author in preparation for a mid-career seminar at George Washington University. This survey was conducted in person and on line in 2012. The 21st Century Leadership Skills Seminar was subsequently organized with the Smithsonian Institution and GWU Museum Studies and held at GWU from 2014 to 2016. Results of an April 2017 survey of thirty-three emerging museum professionals with master's degrees in Museum Studies corroborated the same list of skills as critical to their success in the workplace.

9. BOP consulting, "Character Matters: Attitudes, Behaviours and Skills in the UK Museum Workforce," September 2016, http://www.artscouncil.org.uk/sites/default/files/download-file/ACE_Museums_Workforce_ABS_BOP_Final_Report.pdf.

10. Marsha L. Semmel, "Six Skills for Leaders at All Levels," *Museum* (May/June 2015): 65–66.

11. Martha Morris, "1995 Survey of Strategic Planning, Organizational Change and Quality Management," informal benchmarking study of twenty-nine US museums for the Smithsonian Institution, National Museum of American History.

12. Jo Haas, "You're One: Identifying and Developing New Leaders," *Hand to Hand* 29, no. 3 (2015): 13–14.

13. Joel Stinnett, "How the Kentucky Science Center Is Pushing Creative Development," *Louisville Business Journal,* June 9, 2017, https://www.bizjournals.com/louisville/news/2017/06/09/how-the-kentucky-science-center-is-pushing.html.

14. Email exchange between Jo Haas and the author, June 21, 2017.

15. Alex Randall, "Executive Director Roadmap: Insights into OCMA's Lori Fogarty," blog post, http://www.emergingsf.org/heart-lori-fogarty-executive-director-oakland-museum/

16. Peter F. Drucker, *Managing the Nonprofit Organization* (New York: HarperCollins, 1990), 201.

17. Frank Sofia, "Millennial Leaders Are Here: What Will Change and How to Manage It," *Forbes,* March 15, 2017, https://www.forbes.com/sites/

sap/2017/03/15/millennial-leaders-are-here-what-will-change-and-how-to -manage-it/#7c3b67ed4399.

18. Nathan Ritchie, "Career Path: Educator-Turned Director," *Museum* 96, no. 1 (2017): 17.

19. Nexus LAB, "Layers of Leadership across Libraries, Archives and Museums," https://educopia.org/deliverables/nexus-lab-layers-leadership -across-libraries-archives-and-museums-september-2016-draft.

20. Michael E. Shapiro, *Eleven Museum Directors* (Atlanta: High Museum of Art, 2015), 56.

21. Carol Dweck and Kathleen Hogan, "How Microsoft Uses a Growth Mindset to Develop Leaders," *Harvard Business Review*, October 5, 2016, https://hbr.org/2016/10/how-microsoft-uses-a-growth-mindset-to-develop -leaders.

22. Wendy C. Blackwell, "Career Path: Transferable Skills," in *A Life in Museums: Managing Your Museum Career*, ed. Greg Stevens and Wendy Luke (Washington, DC: American Association of Museums, 2012), 130–132.

23. Michael Beer, Magnus Finnstrom, and Derek Schrader, "Why Leadership Training Fails—and What to Do about It," *Harvard Business Review* 94, no. 10 (2016): 50–57.

24. See Getty Leadership Institute, https://gli.cgu.edu and Clore Leadership program, https://www.cloreleadership.org.

25. John Wenzel, "MCA Denver Wins $400,000 Grant for National Leadership Program," *Denver Post*, February 3, 2017, http://www.denverpost .com/2017/02/03/mca-denver-grant-museums-programs/.

26. Author conversation with Lauren Telchin-Katz, April 4, 2017.

27. Author conversation with Allison Titman, March 10, 2017.

28. Email exchange between Jessica Nicoll and the author, April 19, 2017.

29. AAMD demographic survey 2015, https://mellon.org/programs/ arts-and-cultural-heritage/art-history-conservation-museums/demographic -survey/.

30. Hillary M. Sheets, "Pressure Mounts for US Museums to Increase Diversity at the Top," *Art Newspaper*, August 3, 2017, http://theartnewspaper .com/news/museums/pressure-mounts-for-us-museums-to-increase-diversity -at-the-top.

31. Joan R. Baldwin and Anne W. Ackerson, *Women in the Museum: Lessons from the Workplace* (New York: Routledge, 2017), 56–59.

32. Susan Chira, "Why Women Aren't C.E.O.s, According to Women Who Almost Were," *New York Times*, July 23, 201, https://www.nytimes .com/2017/07/21/sunday-review/women-ceos-glass-ceiling.html.

33. Laura Huerta-Migus, lecture delivered at the Museum Studies University Seminar, April 27, 2017.

34. LA County Museum of Art, Press Release, November 29, 2016, at http://www.lacma.org/sites/default/files/2016-Mellon-Undergraduate -Curatorial-Fellowship- press-release-11.29.16_0.pdf.

35. Robin Pogrebin, "De Blasio, with 'Cultural Plan,' Proposes Linking Money to Diversity," *New York Times*, July 20, 2017, https://mobile.nytimes .com/2017/07/19/arts/design/new-york-cultural-plan-museums.html?emc =edit_th_20170720&nl=todaysheadlines&nlid=32038473&referer.

36. Frank Dobbin an Alexandra Kalev, "Why Diversity Programs Fail," *Harvard Business Review* 94, no. 7 (2016): 52–60.

37. Brian Boucher, "From Interns to the Boardroom New York's Museums Need to Diversify," Artnet.com, July 31, 2017, https://news.artnet.com/ art-world/board-room-new-york-museums-diversity-1034267#.WX _QU1yPW5M.

38. Isaac Kaplan, "Gender Gap Wider at Wealthier Museums, New Study Finds," *Artsy*, March 23, 2017, https://www.artsy.net/article/artsy-editorial -gender-gap-wider-wealthier-museums-new-study-finds.

39. Geraldine Kendall, "Museums and Their Staff Are Paying the Price of Low Wages," *Museums Journal*, Museums Association 116, no. 6 (2016): 12–13, https://www.museumsassociation.org/museums-journal/news-analysis/ 01062016-museums-and-their-staff-are-paying-the-price-of-low-wages.

LEADERSHIP IN ACTION

CASE STUDIES

his text has delved into the challenges of leadership in museums today with a focus on best practices of organizations and individuals, harnessing the change process, implementing innovative approaches, and preparing the next generation. The book has highlighted the great contributions of a variety of leaders in the field who have made an impact. In this chapter the reader will find more detailed case studies of leadership in action. Clearly there are many individuals and organizations who could be a part of this text as creative leaders exist across the country and around the world. Many are engaged in transformative work and sharing their stories through professional conferences, blog sites, teaching, mentoring, and publications. This chapter then is a snapshot of what is happening today through the lens of several individuals making a difference. As leadership occurs at all levels of the organization, these case studies include contributions of both executive directors and those leading at lower levels. Several of these case studies feature leaders at different stages of their careers. All are engaged in a process of change for their organization and making an impact in their communities. In some cases the transformative work described is ongoing; in others, it captures a history of important accomplishments. Although it would be convenient to identify leadership styles of these individuals, it is best to say that each is adaptive, empathetic, pragmatic, and self-aware. The case studies represent varied types and sizes of museums including a historic site, and history, art, children's, university, specialized, and multidisciplinary museums. I am pleased that several of these individuals were willing to respond *in their own words* to key questions about their work, and to talk about their own personal leadership journeys and the skills they feel are most critical to success in the museum field. Above all these cases are remarkable examples of values-based leadership. The following organizations are featured in this chapter

- President Lincoln's Cottage
- Cincinnati Museum Center
- Senator John Heinz History Center
- American University Museum at the Katzen Arts Center
- EdVenture Children's Museum
- Musical Instrument Museum
- Albright-Knox Art Gallery
- Virginia Historical Society
- Smithsonian Institution

Washington, DC's, *President Lincoln's Cottage* under the leadership of Erin Carlson Mast has produced groundbreaking public programs in support of social justice issues, built a new 501(c)(3) organization, and achieved LEED certification in their historic restoration. As a unique national landmark and historic site, the Cottage has been recognized at the highest levels for its impact. The Cottage's story written by Erin Mast follows.

President Lincoln's Cottage

Erin Carlson Mast, CEO and Executive Director

President Lincoln's Cottage and the adjacent Robert H. Smith Visitor Education Center opened to the public for the first time in 2008, giving Americans an intimate, never-before-seen view of Abraham Lincoln's presidency and family life. The grand opening was made possible following a $15,000,000 restoration and rehabilitation of both buildings and the surrounding landscape under the auspices of the National Trust for Historic Preservation, a private, nonprofit organization. Since January 1, 2016, the site has been managed and operated by President Lincoln's Cottage at the Soldiers' Home, a 501(c)(3) public charity with a governing board of directors. President Lincoln's Cottage is designated a National Monument (2000), National Historic Landmark (1974), and site of the National Trust for Historic Preservation, but receives no federal operating support.

Community Engagement Programs

As a National Monument with a global message located in a very residential part of Washington, DC, our site serves local, national, and international audiences. President Lincoln's Cottage is located in a neighborhood where demographics have changed dramatically since the capital project launch in 2001. Our neighborhood has become younger, more affluent, and more diverse. We emphasize collaborating with the communities we serve, and look for connections that transcend individual experience while drawing strength from it.

President Lincoln's ideas provide an ideal foundation for engaging such a diverse audience through our programs. Our team is trained to facilitate conversations amongst visitors with opposing political views, who come from a variety of cultures, and represent a spectrum of ages and knowledge levels. Lincoln's experience with people in DC shaped his views and decisions, but those very decisions had national and international impact, impact that also transcends time. The story of his leadership allows us to address contemporary humanitarian concerns that have specific historical and local examples from which we can draw. By being in touch with the needs and concerns of our audience, and being mindful of our competencies and purpose, we are better positioned to serve an evolving audience while staying true to our mission.

Strategic Partnerships

As a small organization in a region awash with nonprofits serving a vast array of functions, we relish the opportunities to nurture partnerships and collaborations aligned with our purpose. Our relationships with other museums, educational institutions, and nonprofits run the gamut from extended, formal partnerships that continue to grow to one-time marketing collaborations. For example, we found a stellar cultural fit with Polaris, a leading anti-human trafficking NGO, that aligns with our focus on the historical arc of slavery. What started as a one-time collaboration grew into a robust partnership in which we engage with one another through meeting spaces, tours, speaking engagements, exhibits, and more. The affinity between our organizations became so strong that it led, without any conflict or angst, to a shared board member and shared donors.

A more traditional museum partnership is with the Civil War Washington Museum Consortium, which includes President Lincoln's Cottage, Ford's Theatre Society, Frederick Douglass House, and Tudor Place. The consortium hosts annually two week-long teacher workshops each summer. Our organizations vary in budget, staffing, size, and location, but each participates in a complementary way that doesn't rely on a balance sheet to define what constitutes an equitable contribution to the effort. The system works and feedback attests that teachers are getting exponentially more out of the experience by interacting with all four organizations as a team. Our most successful partnerships reflect a cultural fit between the organizations, an absence of ego, respect for what each group brings to the table, and results that advance our mission.

Programs and the Historic Facility

Our philosophy is to respect the authenticity of this place and to embrace the power and context the history provides for our community. That includes being honest about what we do, what we do not know, and sharing complex and uncomfortable stories with everyone in age-appropriate ways. Our mandate evolved from being a Museum of Ideas, to serving as the Home for Brave Ideas. Every year we welcome and engage individuals and organizations, such as the Center for Inspired Teaching or American Immigration Council, who are carrying out Lincoln's unfinished work. They tell us that being here provides inspiration and space for transformative reflection. We have come to embrace our role of being a secular site of pilgrimage—a crucible of change for the past and present. Programs we hosted during the 2016 presidential election cycle, such as the UNITY project and an evening of reflection on November 9, exemplified this.

In the 2010s, "The Period of Significance Is Now" gained strength as a mantra in preservation and public history. The phrase encapsulates what our organization and others had been practicing for some time. Isolating ourselves from the past by focusing on a static "period of significance" falls short if you believe the past has a direct impact on our present and future. We challenge ourselves to infuse our entire operation—not just our interpretive programming—with our mission in deliberate ways, improving each year. From our HR practices, to sourcing our museum store merchandise, to our agreements with contractors, we find ways to ensure we are continuing the fight for freedom and supporting others in their efforts through the business choices we make. For example, we launched a campaign for certified-slavery-free floor coverings for the Cottage over a more historically accurate material made under potentially questionable conditions. This may seem like common sense, but in a field that prizes accuracy, it was actually a conscious departure from the normal criteria for preservation decision making. From a big picture standpoint, it is perfectly in keeping with our mission. It's a decision that was more authentic to who we are as an organization.

We are mindful of best practices and trends, but if they do not work for us and cannot be adapted to our operation responsibly, we don't pursue them. After all, flexibility and creativity are best practices, too.

Rapid Prototyping

In many ways, we've employed rapid-prototyping from our inception. The capital restoration project included a great deal of studies and prototyping to create a new model of preservation and interpretation. Those results underscored the need for adaptable systems and methods. While we planned to design multipurpose spaces and systems where possible, it was obvious that the most adaptable resource was our team. By focusing on robust training and professional development, we are positioned to give our people the freedom to respond effectively, thoughtfully, and creatively to situations as they arise, and to learn from the results.

Two examples exemplify how this works in practice. The first example addressed a preservation challenge. Senior Preservationist, Jeffrey

Larry, had observed the failures of textbook cyclical maintenance to keep the Cottage veranda stairs in good repair. We budgeted for a larger investment for the following year. In the meantime, he tested different techniques and products on different stairs. To the visitor, it all looks essentially the same. But the short-term solution allows us to track each technique and application and compare data before we make a more substantial investment. It also allows us to share our results, both failed techniques and successful ones, with the field.

A second example is our tour platform. People often ask if the tour, our longest-running program that serves more individual visitors than any other program we offer, has changed since we opened in 2008. The answer is yes and no. The tour is, at its core, still a conversation based on the power of this place. The focus is still on ideas versus decorative arts. Yet everything else has been modified regularly over time either in response to internal or external changes or in anticipation of them with rapid prototyping. The core tour was created for flexibility, allowing us to test spin-off tours, tours of different lengths, multisensory experiences, new media, different group sizes, evening tours, and more with relative ease. When the changes did not work we either retested with different conditions or moved on to the next tweak. When something works, we scale it as best we can. So yes, the visitor experience and the operation have changed continuously, but in ways that may only be perceptible if you are here infrequently. Rapid prototyping is not to be confused with triage, but rapid prototyping is also a way in which we triage unforeseen problems that do surface. And while the idea and implementation should be something you can execute in short order, there can and sometimes should be a gap between idea and implementation if the timing is not right.

The Challenge of Diversity

Diversity has been an important issue for our organization from the start given the history of what Lincoln accomplished at the Cottage. As a National Monument in Washington, DC, we're mindful and deliberate in our approach to creating an inclusive environment, and one way we achieve that is by continually working toward being a diverse organization. Our partners provide recommendations and help spread the word about board and staff openings so that we are not relying on our network alone. We've enjoyed greater diversity, as defined by typical HR criteria, than many sister sites for some time. While the diversity of our city naturally helps, our commitment to truth telling and a supportive work culture helps us attract and retain diverse talent. As a Lincoln site, we're also proud of our political and geographic diversity, which has proven valuable and essential year after year. Diversity of perspective—influenced by many factors—has been the most important to our work.

Having a diverse staff brings its own challenges. While the field has a great deal of information on training staff to navigate diverse audiences, there is a dearth of information on training a diverse staff to cope with all manner of racist, ageist, and sexist comments from visitors, donors, and other stakeholders. We have provided facilitated trainings on dealing with micro aggressions and in conscious and unconscious biases. We also have held open forums to discuss current events and how politics can impact interaction with all stakeholders. Trainings like these offer support to our team and improve interactions with all our audiences.

Building the Team

As a small museum that is twice a start-up—first when we opened to the public in 2008 and again when we launched our own nonprofit organization in 2016—we recognize how much we have benefited from being nimble, adapting through calculated risks, having a degree of team stability, and a high degree of openness about what we do.

Given that our entire programmatic framework is designed around conversations as means of promoting interconnectedness and trust, it's perhaps unsurprising that our team welcomes a conversational approach internally, too. There are a number of elements of older models of organizational communication, such as speeches to the staff, that we never implemented. We are a relatively small team with fewer than twenty full-time and part-time employees. Being open seven days a week means schedules never perfectly overlap, which necessitates efficient, open lines of communication.

While we continue to experiment with various platforms for internal communication beyond email, we have a basic structure in place that allows for both open and confidential conversations and feedback.

For example, I am empowered by the board to lead our team. I take my responsibility as a coach and mentor seriously, and work to create a learning environment so our team grows through preparation and new challenges. Weekly staff meetings are kept brief—typically thirty minutes—and focus on shared challenges or projects that impact multiple team members. We also implemented different feedback models, including "stay interviews" that identify why people stay and where we can potentially improve.

Building the confidence and knowledge of our entire team has tangible results. For example, our frontline staff—the ultimate storytellers—engage with potential donors, elected officials, teachers, and members of the press often and with great effect. Our director of programming, Callie Hawkins, ensures they are supported in their efforts with ample training, and a structure that prioritizes quality over quantity. Colleagues at other sites have said they would cringe at the idea of their guides speaking with potential donors or the press, but without exception, those same colleagues also express concern over their training program—or lack thereof. How can we expect our team to be good ambassadors and to feel passionate about our mission, when they aren't prepared? By empowering people at appropriate levels, our small organization is able to engage more people both more personally and more effectively than if we strictly limited those kinds of interactions to senior staff or the board.

Nonprofit Employment Challenges

As the Cradle of the Emancipation Proclamation, fair labor practices are a pillar of our work. It is just one of the reasons we pay all individuals who work here regularly, rather than relying on volunteers for daily operations. Paying our frontline education staff is not a small investment on our part, but it is a worthwhile one.

As part of our separation from a much larger organization, our board mandated that I make sure our people were as good if not better off with our new organization from a salary and benefits standpoint. That was a tall order given that we went from a 100+ organization to an organization of fewer than 20 full-time equivalent employees. Working closely with our HR provider, we were able to meet the mandate. We had surveys and staff discussions to learn what mattered most to our current team, researched what benefits we needed to offer to be competitive to future employees, and had many discussions about finding the right mix of benefits and providers that offered the best value. We landed in a very good place and are proud of having a progressive handbook and competitive salary and benefits, particularly for a nonprofit of our size. All of that would mean nothing, however, if we didn't do the financial planning to be able to offer our team job stability. It's reasonable to expect that we budget for merit increases and bonuses, that we pay all individuals serving staff functions, and that we pay our interns to diversify the pipeline of people who have essential on-the-job experience. Our goal is to demonstrate that we value people whose talents could earn them more capital in the for-profit sector, but who are drawn to the values and environment our organization provides.

Strategic Planning

For years we have employed a major strategic planning process every five years with rolling three-year plans for the organization that assigns specific tactics and goals to various staff members. The first strategic plan for the independent organization was approved in 2017, and came on the heels of a year of national awards and recognition for our work. As such, it's not surprising that the plan focuses more on honing excellence than overhauling the program. Metrics were an area of intense focus, as we make exciting changes in how we evaluate our success. It is easier to track quantitative metrics than qualitative metrics, but the qualitative metrics are of considerable importance to us. For example, many sites are focused on the number of visitors they get in a year. That's a metric that's nearly universal and is surely important, but it reveals nothing about engagement and depth of impact.

We set out to create a transformative experience, but some of the measures of that—memberships, book sales, third-party review sites—were peripheral. Visitors were independently reaching out to us weeks, months, even years later to tell us their experience at President Lincoln's Cottage had stayed with them and changed them in some way. What we were not sure of is whether that was statistically significant, or merely anecdotal. To find out, Hawkins reached out to the Academy of Neuroscience for Architecture in 2014. We partnered with a member of the Academy to create a new tool that would help us understand the depth of visitor impact. The initial phase of the study, a year-long phenomenological study, launched in 2016. Ideally, this will be followed by a more in-depth neuroscientific study.

The Facility and the Mission

Our mission reflects our facility. We have the power of an authentic historic space where people are inspired to take up Lincoln's unfinished work in different ways and on many levels. We embrace the responsibility to reflect our mission in how we use the space. We choose programming that uses the space for both serious discussions, such as when we host partner nonprofits dealing with humanitarian crises, as well as relaxing but informational events, such as our Cottage Conversations program or Two-Faces Comedy series. We also make sure we're being responsible stewards, which means excellence in preservation, a commitment to green practices, and a commitment to corporate responsibility. For example, our Robert H. Smith Visitor Education Center, a rehabilitated 1905 building, is LEED Gold certified. Our museum store features merchandise that advance our mission, including products made by survivors of human trafficking.

Financial Sustainability

We deal with financial realities by facing them head-on through budgeting and planning processes. President Lincoln's Cottage opened to the public in 2008—a historically difficult economic year—without an endowment. Through rigorous planning and disciplined budgeting, we've managed incremental growth and the creation of a cash reserve fund. When we began discussing the prospect of spinning off as an independent 501(c)(3) organization in earnest, I worked with consultants to develop a Financial Feasibility study for our organization. The study included high, medium, and low estimates of additional costs of running our organization independently and three projections of our performance from the grimmest to the rosiest.

With the plan in place, we were able to budget responsibly, focus our fundraising efforts, and get board buy-in prior to launching our own nonprofit. Knowing that we can withstand major revenue shocks gives us the stability to think clearly and avoid a scarcity mind-set. It allows us to keep our focus on thriving rather than merely surviving.

Qualities of Transformative Leaders

Lincoln is by far one of the most influential transformative leaders our country has produced, and this is where he developed some of his most transformative decisions. I particularly admire three timeless qualities of Lincoln that I feel are important to transformational leadership: Authenticity, Openness, and Determination. Authenticity requires knowing who you are as much as knowing who you aren't. It's about earning the credibility to do the work well. Openness includes the trifecta of awareness, dialogue, and transparency. Determination is about maintaining focus and drive, and refusing to pass the buck. Those three qualities are interrelated. For example, without Openness, you risk losing Authenticity. Ultimately the qualities are about how you relate to everyone around you versus qualities you can control in a vacuum.

░ ░ ░

The *Cincinnati Museum Center* was created from the merger of three existing museums in the 1990s and has developed a fine reputation for programs and community responsiveness. Housed in the historic Union Terminal the museum provides programming in science, natural history, regional history, and children's programming. Elizabeth Pierce represents a CEO who worked her way up from middle management to the executive suite. Pierce assumed the lead role in 2015. Her case study highlights lessons learned along the way including the importance of mentorships. The following profile is based on an interview with the author.

Cincinnati Museum Center

Elizabeth Pierce, CEO and President

Selecting an internal candidate for the top position in a museum is not common. However, in some cases there is an obvious internal candidate who can ascend to the position in a smooth transition. Unlike many young museum professionals Pierce had an early interest in leadership, early childhood development, and philanthropy. After receiving her MA in Museum Studies in 1995 she landed her first job at Chicago Children's Museum in a marketing and development position. When her family moved to Cincinnati in 2001, she sought an opportunity to work in public relations. Many of her clients were nonprofits, including Cincinnati Museum Center. Working with then CEO Douglass McDonald, she was appointed to the CMC's Duke Energy Children's Museum's advisory board. As chair of the advisory board she worked closely with the CMC Board of Trustees. This gave her a unique view of the museum's stakeholders and the operations of the organization. She was eventually offered a position on the staff as head of marketing and development. Pierce notes that it was important to ask to be "at the leadership table." Working closely with the board and CEO she was in a position to be coached in various leadership skills. One area that was important was financial competency. Pierce was at the museum during a pivotal time when they were lobbying to receive taxpayer funding to support the renovation of their historic Union Terminal facility. CMC was also moving to merge with the National Underground Railroad Museum and Freedom Center. Pierce played key roles in both of these initiatives. When CEO McDonald announced his retirement in 2014 she was named Chief Operating Officer. Subsequently she became interim CEO working closely with the board chair.

Due to the exceptional job she was doing along with her considerable knowledge of the organization she was name CEO in 2015. The museum did not have a formal succession plan, yet it was clear that Pierce was a logical candidate to assume the role. As many new leaders do, she felt the need to make changes. These included filling positions that had become vacant, adding a new CFO, and a chief learning officer. She also turned over the fundraising mantle to a new vice president for advancement. Pierce then became more closely engaged in the core programmatic areas of collections, curatorial, and exhibitions as key components of the new visitor experience. Expanding program development to add STEM to the range of natural history, regional history, and child development is a strategic priority as they renovate and reopen the historic facility. The opportunity to demonstrate how all of these areas can intersect and overlap is the unique proposition that makes this moment so exciting for Pierce.

Pierce is an advocate of staff support and development. She invests in staff attendance at professional conferences and she encourages more learning in the area of visitor services and competency training. After conducting a staff engagement survey, she learned that some staff were uncertain of their roles. This is often the case with leadership change as well as a major renovation program. Her charge is to continue to provide support and to coach staff to be more risk taking. She will be reinforcing the museum's strategic plan, with the top priorities for CMC including the building renovation and the new exhibitions in the renovated spaces. A capital campaign will raise funds for the latter along with an operating endowment. In considering the requirements of an effective leader Pierce emphasizes the importance of community engagement and political advocacy. These are balanced with a focus on internal alignment and competency building. To stay engaged with broad leadership trends she joined a CEO roundtable representing a variety of organization in the city which is a great way to pursue peer learning.[1]

Pittsburgh's *Senator John Heinz History Center* has used rapid prototyping to develop their public programming. In the following case study Vice President Sandra Smith details their work in developing a new program that features a public-private partnership. In addition Smith shares her thoughts on best practices in leadership along with her career trajectory, which includes prior positions in collections management and as a small museum director.

Senator John Heinz History Center: Program Development

Sandra Smith, Vice President Engagement & Enterprise

The Senator John Heinz History Center traces its roots back to 1879, making it the oldest cultural institution in Western Pennsylvania. The museum system includes the Western Pennsylvania Sports Museum, the Thomas & Katherine Detre Library & Archives, the Fort Pitt Museum, and the Meadowcroft Rockshelter and Historic Village. With the opening of the Smithsonian wing in 2004, the History Center became the largest history museum in Pennsylvania. The new wing allows better opportunities found in our affiliation with the Smithsonian Institution. The additional space added the Western Pennsylvania Sports Museum, the Mueller Education Center, the Special Collections Gallery, and the McGuinn Gallery for traveling exhibitions. The 370,000-square-foot museum presents compelling stories from American history with a Western Pennsylvania connection in an interactive environment perfect for visitors of all ages. The History Center is a 501(c)(3) governed by a board of fifty-seven, and has approximately eighty full and part-time staff, as well as another fifty seasonal or hourly staff. The organization's budget is approximately $9,000,000 dollars annually.

On Rapid Prototyping

We use this approach most often in designing new public programs. While we haven't necessarily created a strict process, most of our new program development involves the followings steps:

- *Idea Generation:* identify an audience segment that has potential for growth and conceive a program based on current knowledge of public trends and needs, relation to the institution's mission, collaborative brainstorming with multiple museum departments, and availability of resources.
- *Partnerships:* identify potential program partners—nonprofit or for-profit—that can enhance or assist in program development, and that already have favorable brand recognition. Criteria for partnerships can include the ability to reach new audiences through the partner; the capacity to take on part of the program development that they may be better equipped to do; or other mutual benefit.
- *Marketing:* establish an appropriate marketing mix in order to most effectively reach relevant audiences. Create a program description and promotional materials that are engaging and share-worthy. All messaging should be consistent with the institution's overarching brand persona.
- *Lifespan:* recognize that any new program or community engagement tool has a finite lifespan under even the best of circumstances; this helps reduce the "fear factor" of trying to permanently address a need or solve a problem.

- *Goal Setting:* identifying and quantifying measures of success as these can be radically different from program to program. For some, attendance is the most important goal; for others, it might be measurable impact, revenue generation, or even media attention.
- *Testing:* hold the initial public program while tracking the stated measures of success through audience evaluation, media monitoring, or attendance and revenue statistics.
- *Review Outcomes:* quickly following the program, hold a debriefing session to review the outcomes with all involved parties, then identify steps for refinement or improvement.
- *Monitoring:* for annual or repeated programs, compare year over year outcomes to identify larger trends. These should be contextualized as much as possible. Does the time of year impact program success? The weather? Is the market becoming saturated; in other words, are other museums or organizations doing similar programming? Is general interest in the topic waning? All these factors will help determine when a program needs to be refreshed or abandoned.

One very successful use of this approach was in the development of a large-scale public program called Hometown-Homegrown at the Heinz History Center. Under the guidance of President and CEO Andy Masich, the museum had been moving into more in-depth interpretation and programming around the topic of food and food history in Western Pennsylvania, responding to a growing trend nationally and locally, especially as Pittsburgh was becoming noted more and more for its food scene. The History Center staff spent some time considering ideas for incorporating food programming. We wanted to remain rooted in Pittsburgh history in order to set ourselves apart from some of the other food trends we saw happening locally. Serendipitously, we were approached by a local company called GoodTaste! Pittsburgh about partnering to produce a public program focusing on Pittsburgh's passion for food. GoodTaste! Pittsburgh is a for-profit company that produces popular food shows and expos in the Pittsburgh region. As we explored goals for this potential program, we found a very clear alignment; we both wanted a relaxed, fun, and engaging program that highlighted some of the traditions, foods, and restaurants specific to Pittsburgh. We also realized that the assets the History Center and GoodTaste! Pittsburgh could offer were very complimentary, and the partnership could work well. Specifically, the History Center could offer a unique venue and a great deal of educational content, while GoodTaste! Pittsburgh had contacts throughout the Pittsburgh food scene, and an in-depth knowledge of the management of food shows and the market's interest in them. Ultimately, Hometown-Homegrown was born, and we held our first program in June 2012. The idea was to celebrate Pittsburgh's passion for food by way of a fun and flavorful food show and expo. Museum visitors could expect to sample a delicious assortment of foods from thirty local vendors that represented the best of Pittsburgh's neighborhoods. Additionally, we would offer cooking demonstrations by local celebrity chefs and personalities, access to all five-floors of the History Center's exhibitions, various food-related activities throughout the museum, including scavenger hunts, food and fitness games, a "Pittsburgh's Best Cookie" contest, and a cookbook exchange. Going into it, we had no idea how the program would be received by the public, but we decided to take a chance on the opportunity to try something different with a strong partner. Our goals for the program were simple—to learn how to do a large-scale program based on local food, to gauge the public's interest in food programming, to gain some visibility with new audiences, and with any luck, not lose too much money.

The morning of the program, we all had that "what if nobody comes?" dread, since the program was such a departure from our typical offerings. But above all else, we went into this program knowing it was going to be a learning experience; no matter what happened, we'd gain valuable insight. Luckily, before the museum even opened, the line to get into the building was down the block. The day was exhilarating, fun, exhausting, and of course, a little chaotic.

In the days following the first Hometown-Homegrown, we held a debriefing session with our partner, our program staff involved in planning, our events crew who helped move the vendors in and out, our volunteer coordinator who had feedback from the volunteers, and our visitor services manager. We found:

- Our attendance was nearly 800 in the five hours of the program, which was one of the largest programs we'd ever had at that point. The team rated that as a success; clearly there was public interest in this type of program.

- Despite the somewhat chaotic feel to the day (which in retrospect was due entirely to the volume of people in the building), everything had run smoothly. Vendor load-in and load-out was quick and simple, visitors and vendors were happy and satisfied, volunteers had fun helping people throughout the building, and there were no significant hiccups. Again, we rated this as a success—yes, we could figure out how to do a food program, especially with the expert input from our partner.
- Although our ability to do evaluation on the fly during public programs was very limited at that time, our staff observed many first-time visitors discussing their likelihood to return to the History Center.
- Because it was our first time doing the program, we had to purchase supplies and print signage, essentially start-up expenses. Although that was offset by admissions revenue, shop revenue, and membership sales during the event, we did still end up a little in the red on the program, but not significantly. Given all the other successes, and with the new understanding that this was the inaugural year of what we hoped would be a long-standing, annual program, we didn't consider this a major negative.
- We identified some refinements we could make the following year. For example, the "Pittsburgh's Best Cookie" contest was a bust. While it earned some media and public interest for the program in advance, it was complicated to manage and didn't add significantly to the program itself. Other refinements were minor—improvements to the cooking demonstrations, the layout of the vendors, and other changes to improve the flow of the program.

In five years, Hometown-Homegrown has become a marquee annual program for the History Center, and has more than doubled in attendance since the first iteration. Every year at our first planning meeting with our partner, we start with a discussion with the topic of current food trends, and from there think critically about what program elements to add or change to keep the program fresh. Each year we have new foods to taste, new vendors, new chefs, and new activities, but key popular elements remain the same: a local television chef with a cult following always does a demonstration, an excellent offering of History Center exhibitions, and our cookbook exchange, which has grown from a small "leave one, take one" table to a full reading library with over a thousand used cookbooks available for exchange or purchase.

In 2016, we decided to move the program from June to October. In looking at the attendance trends and the local event calendars, we recognized that summer in Pittsburgh is packed with competing activities. We also noted that attendance at the program seemed to go up on rainy days over the years, which made us think that our visitors might hesitate to spend a sunny summer day indoors. It also gave us the opportunity to refresh our branding of the program with updated marketing and program elements related to gall. We recognize that—like all programs—Hometown-Homegrown might still have a limited lifespan, but with careful attention, planning, and calculated change and risk-taking, we believe that Hometown-Homegrown will continue to be a marquee public program for the History Center and our partner GoodTaste! Pittsburgh for years to come.

On Leadership Qualities

Support and care for employees as whole people, ensuring they get the opportunity and encouragement for a healthy work/life balance. Make sure they have and take sufficient time off to recharge or to manage responsibilities outside the office. Encourage them to explore personal interests and passions outside the organization; staff will be happier and more fulfilled, and may even bring outside connections and lessons back to the organization, enriching both employee and employer.

Listen, don't dictate. If you've hired correctly, your staff are the experts in their jobs and are on the front lines, and therefore often have information you don't. Let them make decisions, recommendations to you, and give feedback on what's working and what isn't, while you provide strategic direction and context for their work. A leader's job is to clear the staff's path of any roadblocks, allowing them to do what they do best with minimal distraction.

Similarly, we should listen to the community and hear what it is they want from us, rather than provide what we *think* they need. This can take many forms: public sessions in the strategic planning process, private conversations with key stakeholders, and even simply paying attention to attendance data and trends to see how the public is responding.

Embrace failure. Failure is a necessary component of innovation, and we shouldn't be embarrassed about it when it happens. When I finished graduate school, I needed a nonacademic pursuit to fill my newly found free time for a while. I started figure skating, something I'd always wanted to do as a kid. Of course, I was terrified of falling—especially as an adult—but as I became more comfortable with the risks involved, it became less scary. I realized that if I wasn't falling sometimes, I wasn't trying hard enough. Sure, I fell frequently and had the broken bones, scars, and bruises to prove it, but I learned that I'd heal and that landing that scary jump was definitely worth the pain and embarrassment of flailing around on the ice. It's important to celebrate our successes at work; if we don't, morale can become poor and everything suffers. But it's equally important to air out and celebrate our failures so we and others can learn from them, and so they're no longer something to fear.

My Career History

When I went off to college, I majored in the Classics. I studied literature, art, architecture, religion, material culture, and more. I supplemented it with a minor in Art History, which seemed more like social and cultural history than just art. After college, I interned at a local arts organization, then eventually got a job teaching in a school-aged childcare program. The following school year, I became a volunteer teacher and librarian on a reservation in South Dakota, and spent some time there studying Lakota culture. When the year was up I went back to the afterschool program.

Ultimately, I knew teaching wasn't what I wanted to do, and so I leapt at the opportunity to take a job as an office manager in a small museum in Washington, DC. It was the perfect introduction into the museum world; in a small museum, I was able to learn about all facets of museum work—administration, education, curation, collections management, and even the museum shop.

After a year, I began the museum studies program at George Washington University with a focus on collections management. The program requires several internships, and I was fortunate to find a part-time paid internship in collections management at the National Trust for Historic Preservation. I assisted with loans, the collections database, and the insurance and appraisal programs at the National Trust Historic Sites. My internship eventually turned into a full-time position helping to implement and train staff to use a new collections database. It was an exciting job, one that helped me to understand the realities of smaller historic sites and their capacities to manage their museum collections.

After two years in that role, I became the director of Museum Collections for the National Trust. In the next four years, I worked with the National Trust Historic Sites to help manage their collections, to design and implement yet another collections database, and to bring several new historic sites into the National Trust's portfolio. At the time, National Trust Historic Sites ranged from very small museums with minimal staff and low visitation to major historic sites with large staffs and many thousands of visitors annually. It was fascinating to see how many issues in interpretation and management were common to both.

The National Trust had accepted several historic sites that would come to the organization as part of their estate, including Philip Johnson's Glass House in New Canaan, Connecticut, and Villa Finale in San Antonio, Texas. Villa Finale was home to Walter Mathis, a prodigious collector and preservationist. We had the unique opportunity to gather a great deal of information about his life and his collection in the last years of his life. The National Trust hired a collections manager to catalog, photograph, and document his entire 12,000-piece collection. This was a multi-year process, and was nearing completion when Mr. Mathis passed away. That same year, I had the extraordinary opportunity to take part in the Seminar for Historical Administration. In that program, I began to see how a history museum or historic site can have an impact on communities in the present. The story of Mr. Mathis, a contemporary preservationist, was inspiring; through his story, I saw an opportunity to show how one person truly can make a difference in their community. When the National Trust was making plans to convert the home and collection to a historic site, I jumped at the chance to be a part of it. I moved to San Antonio to become the site's founding director.

Over the next several years, we finished cataloging and conserving the collection; created a visitor center with exhibits, a museum shop, and offices; undertook a full renovation of the house itself including accessibility upgrades; created interpretive and operations plans, and managed the five commercial properties that came along with the estate. Given that the museum was in the heart of a very engaged neighborhood, one of my major responsibilities was building collaborative and trusting relationships with our neighbors. The museum opened to the public in 2010.

After a year of operations, and nearly ten intense years on the project, I realized it was time to hand the reins over to someone with fresh energy and fresh ideas. I left Villa Finale and took a position at the Heinz History Center in Pittsburgh, Pennsylvania. Having spent five years at a small historic site, I was ready to be part of the staff at a much larger history museum. My position at the History Center was primarily focused on education and public programs, while also overseeing visitor services, the museum shop, and our facility rental program. Gradually, as the education and program departments strengthened, my role shifted more towards earned income and other enterprise operations. I focused on reinforcing the already robust earned income programs, building them to the point where they provide about a quarter of our operating budget. Lessons learned from the earned income programs also began to feed back into our programming departments, and helped us to develop a more business-like approach to planning and implementing public programs. Recently, our very active publications program and the museum's marketing and communications were added to my role, which allows for even more collaboration and coordination across departments. While time will tell where this opportunity will lead, it's been exciting challenging assumptions and developing new approaches to all areas of this work!

※ ※ ※

Washington, DC's, *American University Museum* under the leadership of Jack Rasmussen has become a vibrant arts space and teaching facility. Rasmussen is a nimble and visionary leader with skills in many areas. This case study outlines numerous ways that a skilled leader and seasoned risk taker can work effectively within a larger organization to build a unique resource for the community. The following profile is based on an interview with the author.

American University Museum at the Katzen Arts Center

Jack Rasmussen, Director and Curator

Jack Rasmussen has had a distinguished career over several decades as a curator and director running a variety of galleries and museums. A multitalented individual, Rasmussen has degrees in Fine Arts, Anthropological Linguistics, and Arts Management. This combination is unique and exactly right for the work he does. He is a practicing artist, he understands the social dynamics of individuals and communities, and has a penchant for raising money, dealing with boards and collectors, and a sense of what the market needs. He has started alternative arts spaces, run his own art gallery, served as a museum educator and a fundraising officer. Rasmussen is not afraid to learn and stretch. One of the most important accomplishments of his career is having created an artistic dialogue among cultures, countries, generations, and art lovers. His attention to local artists of the Washington, DC, region is legendary, having established a collecting and exhibition initiative funded by local philanthropist Carolyn Alper. But his work goes well beyond the local community bringing in the views and voices of artists working around the globe.

The definition of Rasmussen's philosophy is evident in the mission of the American University Museum:

- We FOCUS on international art because American University has a global commitment.
- We SHOW political art because the university is committed to human rights, social justice, and political engagement.
- We SUPPORT the artists in our community because the university takes an active and responsible role in the formation of our region's contemporary art and culture.

The museum truly reflects the university's focus. They stage about thirty changing exhibitions a year. Some are created in house while others are borrowed or part of a partnership with other arts organizations. Exhibitions are shown in galleries in the three-story 24,000-square-foot museum as well as a sculpture garden and exterior plaza. The museum is a landmark on the campus and sits at the nexus of a major commuter route. Rasmussen has established a close rapport with local galleries, collectors, museums, and embassies and often collaborates with guest curators. As the museum has a permanent collection of 6,000 art works and expects that number to more than double with the impending accessioning of 7,000 works from the now-defunct Corcoran Gallery of Art, the concept of "alternative space" is morphing into a more traditional organization. Having been director for the past dozen years, Rasmussen has developed the programs, built the staff, and raised the funds to achieve an ambitious program. As an adaptive leader, he continues to make strategic connections, to proto-type new ideas, and to lay the groundwork for a growing collection.

Staffing at the museum consists of an assistant director, registrar, preparator, manager of visitor services, marketing and publications specialist, and student assistants and professional contractors. Ras-mussen works with students in the fine arts and arts management programs at AU and is dedicated to developing a new generation of arts professionals. He states "after three years, my staff often moves on to a better job, . . . because they're good, and they get a lot of respon-sibility, and then I'm happy to promote them . . . so, I consider that successful, not a problem." Volunteers are also a part of the mix and they provide support with weekend family programs and other public programs. Working with students also provides for more applications of all aspects of social media, bringing the exhibitions and artists to much wider audiences.

As a university art museum, they are operating on a healthy budget of $1,000,000. Rasmussen raises about 40 percent of this each year. Being embedded in a university allows the museum to participate in major capital campaigns to build new programs and infrastructure capacity. One very prominent result of Rasmussen's fundraising prowess is the $1.5 million Alper Initiative. The donor wished to support local artists through exhibitions, collecting, catalogs, and a unique website.

As a proponent of alternative spaces Rasmussen notes, "basically I'm interested in more contemporary art, but I think it needs to be shown in a context that establishes what came before." In fact he notes that his PhD in Anthropological Linguistics "was just a really great, sort of systematic way of analyzing and compiling contextual information and leading to an interpretation." In his several posi-tions running alternative spaces in DC, Maryland, and California, he has always served as an interpreter and champion of the artist. Each organization allowed him to create new approaches and to build coalitions with collectors, curators, and funders in the community. In DC dominated by federally funded and well-endowed art museums, local artists were adrift. As Washington's Corcoran Gallery of Art headed toward extinction Rasmussen was able to serve the local art community through showcasing these artists alongside those from other parts of the country and the world.

Rasmussen has excelled at risk taking, with a penchant for "provocative" shows. The risky part is sometimes the subject matter (recent shows on Black Lives Matter, Artist Immigrants, the state-sponsored art of North Korea, and the seventieth anniversary of the bombing of Hiroshima and Nagasaki to name a few). Rasmussen often travels abroad to visit artists and galleries and develop ideas for future exhibitions. He spent time in Dubai in advance of organizing a show of Middle Eastern contemporary art. Often trips are paid for by the embassies or other sponsors. He tries to keep flexibility in the exhibitions schedule to accommodate a show that might coincide with a political issue or one of a number of social justice dilemmas.

In the future the museum is poised for a growth spurt, potentially doubling their holdings with the acquisition of collections from the Corcoran Gallery closure. With this added responsibility comes more investment in infrastructure to care for a collection and make it accessible to the public and scholars. In this case the museum, which is now twelve years old, is entering a more mature phase of its life cycle.

The museum is part of a suite of arts programs at American University. Rasmussen reports to the dean of the College of Arts and Sciences, which works well. The university trustees have an interest in the museum and are often helpful in supporting projects. Despite these positive relationships there is a mandate for fundraising and this requires a chunk of the director's time, as much as 30 percent. As they advance to acquiring more collections a new curator and other staff will be hired, giving Rasmussen a chance to work on other projects, and of course raise more money. Fortunately, he has built a cadre of donors who he can call on to help support various projects.

As a director and curator Rasmussen has benefited from networking with colleagues in the university museum field and beyond. Like many successful directors he participated in a regional director's roundtable to provide advice and support. On what the field needs for today, Rasmussen thinks directors need training in management: "In my Arts Management degree, I learned how to read a balance sheet, and you know, . . . that's a must. I also took a course on how bureaucracies work—knowledge you need to survive in a university setting. The key is to keep learning while expanding your cohort of professional contacts. You need every little edge to flourish in this field."[2]

※　※　※

EdVenture in Columbia, South Carolina, is a growing children's museum implementing new approaches to meeting mission including Collective Impact modeling and reaching diverse audiences. Their story is told by former director of special projects Lauren Shenfeld, an emerging museum professional under thirty. The case study emphasizes the importance of empowering staff to do transformative work.

EdVenture Children's Museum

Lauren Shenfeld, Director of Special Projects

Located in South Carolina's capital city, EdVenture opened the doors of its 92,000-square-foot children's museum in downtown Columbia in November 2003, and has since served over 200,000 children and their families annually. As the South's largest children's museum, EdVenture's museum and community-based programming exemplify the organization's mission to "inspire children, youth and the adults who care about them to experience the joy of learning." Interactive exhibitions and state-wide initiatives are developed to support a child's creative thinking, decision-making skills, and increase their sense of self-efficacy, from cradle to career. Operating on an annual budget of approximately $4,000,000, the museum collaborates with schools and direct-service organizations across the state to increase South Carolinian's access to education and health resources.

Leading the charge is CEO Karen Coltrane and an eighteen-member board, which includes three ex officio members who represent EdVenture's key parent and government partners, Richland County and the City of Columbia. The eight-person senior leadership team works closely with Coltrane and the board, and are counted among

EdVenture's thirty-eight full-time employees. Supporting our work in visitor services, summer camps, and our after-school program, *Club EdVenture* has locations during the school year at seven area elementary schools. There are approximately eighty part-time employees.

Serving Community

With nearly 50 percent of our budget devoted to programs that happen outside of the museum's walls and across the state of South Carolina, EdVenture has a heightened awareness of our community's demographics, and our state's increasing diversity. As a museum dedicated to education enrichment and health access for children and their families, we have the flexibility to partner with a range of organizations—from statewide healthcare companies, the University of South Carolina, and city and county government agencies, to school districts and the South Carolina Department of Education, to name a few. EdVenture also consciously partners with organizations dedicated to specific minority communities in South Carolina (for example, our growing Latino community). In total, we have over 300 community partners. Many of these partners' leaders have seats on EdVenture's board, or serve in other volunteer capacities, which promotes initiatives that are responsive to our community's changing demographics.

EdVenture's motto, "Education. Everyone." effectively encompasses our underlying philosophy as it impacts our facility, exhibitions, and public programs. Inside the museum, our facility design, exhibitions, and public programs are literally accessible to all children and their caregivers, often including labels in both English and Spanish, and designed to accommodate children and their caregivers living with disabilities.

Using Innovation

EdVenture's recent approach to successfully responding to community needs is via Collective Impact modeling—a social impact strategy for locally driven, community development that emphasizes a cross-sector and tiered work model of action with a central leadership group (a "backbone" organization), mutually agreed-upon and shared data across parties, and shared goals. Collective impact initiatives have grown in popularity, and been proven successful in the public health and education sectors. In the spring of 2017, EdVenture submitted a grant proposal to the Institute of Museum and Library Services to apply the best practices in collective impact in a two-year, community-centered effort to identify local assets, bring together a unique cross-section of city stakeholders, and develop a locally driven action plan that addresses the pressing and interrelated issues of youth development and gang activity in Hartsville, South Carolina—the site of one of our new satellite museums. Should the grant funding be awarded, following the direction of a collective impact model, the museum will serve as the project's backbone organization, and together with the City of Hartsville's development team, convene leaders in city and neighborhood management, youth counseling, law enforcement, local foundations, religious lay leaders, and K-12, continuing, and higher education administrators to address the city's youth gang violence—a community challenge most museums would not see as their place to help tackle. Even without the funding, EdVenture plans to continue with city management to serve as a neutral and dedicated community convener—a role the museum has successfully played among school professionals and local education stakeholders in the federally designated South Carolina Promise Zone.

The Museum's Focus on Diversity

While EdVenture's emphasis on statewide community outreach underscores the institution's commitment to diversity, so does the makeup of the board and staff. Moreover, because EdVenture serves a diverse community of children and families, we are very intentional in our hiring practices: it is important to us that the staff members with whom our children and families interact are not only high-quality educators, but similarly diverse in gender, race, ethnicity, and even life experiences.

EdVenture's organization-wide initiative, *Yes, Every Child,* also underscores our organization's commitment to diversity. *Yes, Every Child* promotes accessibility to educational programming for under-resourced children and families through targeted community outreach and reduced museum admission: families who are enrolled in the USDA's Supplemental Nutrition Assistance Program or Women, Infants, and Children program, or who receive Medicaid benefits, can come to the museum for just $1 per person. Regardless of cultural, ethnic, geographic, or socio-economic barriers, we believe that every child should have the opportunity to participate in and grow from the unique educational experiences of EdVenture. These efforts are made possible by corporate sponsorships and individual contributions.

Teambuilding, Transparency, and Adaptability

All employees subscribe to a creed referred to as the *EdVenture Way*— the actualization of our four core values: service, honesty, innovation, and joy. When I joined EdVenture as director of Museum Experiences, I inherited a floor staff culture that was relatively negative and nontransparent. With our new CEO's support, and guidance from my supervisor, our executive vice president—who had been the museum's most positive and creative force for nearly ten years—I developed a training for our staff, particularly our visitor services and education teams, adapted from *Learning Together*, created by Boston Children's Museum and Chicago Children's Museum. While *Learning Together* is centered on guest services and creating educational impact in programming, I expanded our training series to include full days of team-building activities, training on adaptability and guest services, meeting with key sponsors and donors, and site visits to our after-school programs. The on-boarding experience also includes transparent discussions with our senior leadership team on our budgets (expenses and revenue goals), program challenges, and the strategic vision for EdVenture. As a young museum leader, it was challenging to build a new community culture and to manage staff members who did not willingly embrace the *EdVenture Way* or our new training philosophy. Nevertheless, I persisted.

Strategic Planning

As we enter our third year with a new CEO, and our second year with a new board chair, the leadership team has embarked on an organization-wide strategic planning process. Until now—with the exception of a grant-funded strategic planning project about five years ago—the majority of our strategic planning has been conducted at a department level on an annual basis. In the Education Department, for example, I completed a comprehensive "Education Plan," which serves as our strategic framework for the year ahead. The goals outlined in our plan help our department measure our impact and success, whether it be a target number of students reached through school and group programs, or a commitment to develop contracts with new school districts in need of high-quality professional learning. For the 2017–2018 programming and fiscal year, we are also excited to launch a longitudinal study with the University of South Carolina, funded by the National Science Foundation, evaluating our youth volunteer program (Museum Apprentice Program) and its impact on minority and low-income students' school success and relationship with STEM subjects. The study will also evaluate the impact of our youth educators on visitor learning. When we have sponsorship or grant support for a new program or initiative, we will always utilize the services of professional evaluators.

Mission-Related Programs

Children's museums are a unique sub-set of museums: they are non-collecting institutions. Rather than focus on collecting art or artifacts that reflect our mission, we strive to develop programs, exhibitions, and learning classrooms that reflect the educational needs of our community. The greatest example of this philosophy is the exhibition, *Dalmatian Station*. The exhibition boasts a real, twenty-four-foot fire truck that children can climb into and pretend to drive. Guests of all ages can try on a firefighter's coat and slide down a fire pole. The exhibition is a fun space for play and make-believe, but is also designed to combat South Carolina's extreme house fire death rate. With their caregivers, children can create a fire escape plan for their home, or review fire safety tips like how to check a smoke detector. Through a partnership with the South Carolina State Fire Marshall's Office, we learned that many times children who are trapped inside their home during a fire are afraid to run to the safety of a fully dressed firefighter. To combat that fear, weekday visitors meet and interact with a professional firefighter dressed in their fire-fighting gas mask and gear. By engaging in this exhibit and its interactive elements, families will be more prepared to prevent house fires—and in the event of an emergency, children will be less afraid of those coming to their rescue.

Financial Sustainability

Like many newly built museums, EdVenture was challenged in its early years by the cost of maintaining its building, and then was hurt by the 2008 recession. Our current senior leadership team has introduced new streams of earned revenue, and expanded programs that are both meeting our mission and providing significant income to the museum. One unique, mission-driven form of earned revenue is our satellite expansion. By 2020, EdVenture will operate a children's museum in the tourist-rich, beach city of Myrtle Beach, South Carolina—which also borders some very needy and rural counties of South Carolina—as well as in Hartsville, South Carolina, a city known for its challenges with poverty and violence, but that is home to some large manufacturing corporations, a private college, and the South Carolina Governor's School for Science and Mathematics.

Qualities of Transformative Leaders

I believe that transformative leaders must be positive, inclusive, and strategic systems-thinkers. These are significant qualities to me because I have witnessed the negative effects of leaders who neither enthusiastically rally other colleagues (or donors), meaningfully align their team toward mutual goals, nor carefully calculate financial decisions and spend money on programs and exhibits that are unrelated to the institution's mission and strategic plan. Undoubtedly, museum and nonprofit professionals are often overworked and underpaid, yet are passionate about creating true impact. A transformative leader with the aforementioned qualities can acknowledge others' value, and not only hold them accountable, but enthusiastically support them toward reaching collective goals that surmount organizational challenges and create change inside the museum and outside in the community. No matter the size of a museum, I believe such a transformative leader also deeply understands and can articulate the bigger-picture goals of the organization; he or she maintains a clear idea of the necessary framework both people and programs provide in achieving those goals.

Today's nonprofit leader can continue to adapt to changing workplace expectations by keeping these qualities at the forefront; by putting the right people in the right role, supporting them, and including them and their ideas in defining goals and achieving success. One of the greatest compliments I have ever received was by EdVenture's director of exhibits in response to my ability to get nearly all of our full-time employees to join me at the museum at 6:30 a.m. on a Saturday morning in preparation for EdVenture's annual Youth Summit. "No one else would be able to do this!" he said. I smiled and realized that at the core of that statement was how I managed to—over the course of nearly six months of planning—stay upbeat about the event, assign roles that matched colleagues' strengths, and keep our larger goal of impact at the forefront of everyone's minds, regardless of how exhausting or frustrating the planning process became. I was proud of my ability to empower my colleagues to give their time and energy to an event that culminated the year's youth development programs, and positively influenced the trajectory of over 200 under-resourced teenagers from across South Carolina.

The *Musical Instrument Museum* in Phoenix, Arizona, provides a unique experience for visitors and community. Executive Director April Salomon leads a museum that is responding to community, educating visitors about the power of music, and providing staff and board an opportunity to build systems to measure outcomes and improve operations. With skills in business and nonprofit leadership she is moving the organization forward applying Six Sigma systems as a more flexible approach to planning and operations. Salomon's case study follows.

Musical Instrument Museum

April Salomon, Executive Director

The Musical Instrument Museum (MIM) was founded by Robert J. Ulrich, former CEO and chairman emeritus of Target Corporation. An avid collector of African art and a world museum enthusiast, Ulrich and his friend Marc Felix originated the idea for MIM after a visit to the Musical Instruments Museum in Brussels, Belgium. Their unique vision was to create a museum and collection that affords representation to the music and musical instruments of every country in the world. Using state-of-the-art audiovisual technology to show musical instruments being played in their original cultural context while also delivering their unique sounds, MIM provides a one-of-a-kind experience to museum guests.

A team of expert curators, which included guidance from distinguished ethnomusicologists, organologists, and other field consultants, assembled MIM's unique collection. The bulk of the collection is highlighted in Geographic Galleries that focus on five major global regions. There are also exhibition spaces such as the Target Gallery, which hosts traveling and special exhibitions, and the Artist Gallery, which includes noteworthy musical instruments and artifacts associated with some of the world's leading musicians. The museum opened its doors to great acclaim on April 24, 2010, and has since helped to raise the arts and cultural profile in Phoenix, Arizona.

MIM is a 501(c)(3) nonprofit organization with a governing board of directors, as well as an advisory board from the greater Phoenix community that works in partnership with MIM's Executive Leadership and governing board to further the museum's mission. In addition to receiving support from individuals, foundations, and corporations, MIM has also received grant funding from public sources such as the Arizona Humanities Council, the Phoenix Office of Arts and Culture, and the Arizona Commission on the Arts.

MIM's mission is to enrich our world by collecting, preserving, and making accessible an astonishing variety of musical instruments and performance videos from every country in the world. MIM offers guests a welcoming and fun experience, incomparable interactive technology, dynamic programming, and exceptional musical performances. MIM also fosters appreciation of the world's diverse cultures by showing how we innovate, adapt, and learn from each other to create music—the language of the soul. In just seven years, MIM is ranked among the top twenty museums in the United States and rated the number one attraction in Phoenix three years in a row (TripAdvisor).

Engaging Community

As a young institution, MIM is continuing to build a reputation, working to become a household name, recognized the world over for its distinction among museums and cultural organizations. Such merit ultimately requires sustained support of the community at large, particularly as a newcomer to the arts and culture scene of a growing metropolitan city with nearly 5,000,000 people.

We know that as a global museum, it is important to make our collection and music from around the world accessible to everyone. Through thoughtful interpretation, innovative program development, musical encounters, and strategic partnering, MIM is committed to providing a world-class experience for every guest who visits. These guiding principles are at the core of MIM's mission and continue to be a focus of the organization's effort to remain a vital part of the global community.

Since the museum's founding, it has been clearly understood that community engagement would be a key component to our success, but even more critical, MIM's long-term sustainability. Thus far, we have partnered and collaborated with more than sixty organizations to more deeply engage the community through music-related programs and offerings. For example, signature "experience" events establish MIM as a center of culture and community by celebrating the musical traditions, instruments, dress, cuisine, and history of a particular culture for an entire weekend. With the help of community partners who support such programming, MIM is able to reach audiences it may not otherwise have access to in Phoenix or the region.

While MIM's primary demographics include a healthy population of retired individuals and young families from greater Phoenix, Scottsdale, and surrounding communities, there has been a significant shift towards increased national and international visitation. In 2010–2011, approximately 72 percent of the visiting public included local residents. Over time, we have seen a greater mix of guests from the Midwest, East Coast, the South, Canada, and other parts of the world, which now makes up more than half of MIM's attendance. Thus, the changing demographics have positively impacted the museum by creating greater awareness and shared experiences for all who visit.

Everything at MIM is about the guest experience, which means a great deal of planning is undertaken to ensure the visiting public stays firmly in mind. Common sense, friendly, professional service makes guests feel welcome in an environment that encourages exploration and discovery of music and world cultures. Whether it is accessibility, information kiosks, our Guideport technology, special programs, expanded content displays, global and local cuisine, special exhibitions, museum store merchandise, or other important considerations, every aspect of what we do focuses on supporting the MIM brand and our guests.

Rapid Prototyping and Six Sigma

When your museum is unlike any other in the world and you have only existed for a handful of years, it would be easy to experiment with various programs and activities that seemingly support and fulfill its mission. In doing so, organizations often experience "mission drift," which causes them to stray from their original intent and guiding principles. At MIM, we have endeavored and learned from piloted initiatives that informed subsequent decisions but were ultimately determined to have diverted substantial time and resources away from our core business. To avoid any potential pitfalls in the future, the leadership team instituted a more disciplined approach to vetting new ideas, as well as improving processes already in place.

Deeply embedded in MIM's workplace culture is a Six Sigma methodology that is applied to just about every aspect of our operations, as well as new projects that might be tested to determine their long-term viability and overall fit with institutional objectives. While this proven methodology has been applied more often within industrial sectors and large corporations, MIM was able to successfully adapt Six Sigma principles and tools as part of a continuous effort to achieve stable and predictable process results, while minimizing variables that might compromise intended outcomes. The goals may be simple or ambitious, but in either case, we have found the structured approach of defining, analyzing, and measuring data, then improving, and controlling the results to be beneficial in many ways.

One of MIM's core values is to be ever-changing, which means we will consistently look for ways to improve the guest experience by creating fresh content throughout the galleries, find emerging talent to present in MIM's music theater, deliver fun and accessible programs to our audiences, and welcome as many schoolchildren through our doors as possible. None of this can be accomplished by accident. We have to be intentional in our approach and that includes critical thinking, as well as a commitment to results that are both data-driven and reflect the qualitative aspects of a given program. Though not an exact blueprint of rapid prototyping, so far, Six Sigma has served MIM well in allowing us to improve where needed and even test a new idea to achieve the strongest results.

In order to reach one of MIM's institutional goals of serving 100,000 school and youth tour participants by 2020, we had to undertake practical, as well as strategic measures toward such an important milestone. Assembling core members of our Six Sigma team for what would become a yearlong project, we defined our objective as increasing attendance numbers through paid school tour admissions since a significant portion of MIM's field trip participants are underserved schoolchildren and youth groups whose admissions are already supported by grant subsidies. Slower summer months also provided an opportunity to welcome more kids given that the majority of field trips occur in the spring and fall.

The Six Sigma team utilized various tools in their approach, including an Effort/Impact matrix, which is used to help determine an implementable solution that is easiest (least *effort* or low hanging fruit) while having the most favorable *impact*. We also looked at ways to improve tour logistics, museum guide support, and parking for school buses in order to accommodate increased numbers over time. During the initial phases of the project, we learned a great deal about Title 1 versus non–Title 1 schools with the former having the greatest need in the state of Arizona. It was clear that charter schools and others that could afford MIM's field trip admissions would remain disproportionate based on the ongoing challenges our state faces with education. While we were able to make some progress with paid admissions (10%) within a year, the real wins occurred when we increased the number of district partnerships across the state, now totaling more than 800 schools. Additional gains in attendance were realized when we stepped up our efforts to reach more youth groups like Boys & Girls Clubs over the summer. In 2017 alone we plan to serve more than 10,000 BGC members between May and August, resulting in a 35 percent increase in school and youth tour admissions overall than the previous year.

Adhering to a Six Sigma methodology can improve results and allow an organization to achieve desired outcomes, which MIM has benefited from time and again.

Building the Team and Communications

MIM takes pride in creating a diverse team of talented, capable, high-performing individuals that have the requisite skills and abilities to bring new ideas, energy, and enthusiasm to the organization. The hiring process, however, is not without rigor or discernment. A combination of interviews at various levels, assessment testing, drug and background screenings, as well as meetings with the executive director and in some cases MIM's founder are all part of building an exceptional team.

Like any other start-up organization, MIM has experienced staffing changes over the years. Team members that were part of the formative phases of the museum's development moved on and were replaced by others, as is a natural process for any new business. In the years that have followed, we have placed greater emphasis on ensuring prospective team members fit well within the organization, can add value, bring a positive attitude to their work, and have the requisite talent, skills, and experience for a particular role. Do they have a passion for music? Are they able to perform in a fast-paced environment? Are they comfortable in a highly collaborative, team atmosphere? Can they adapt quickly to changing business needs? The answers to these questions, among others, can give us a much clearer picture of a candidate's ability to thrive and meaningfully contribute at MIM while working closely with peers, guests, volunteers, and leadership alike. In regard to diversity our organization has had no challenges along these lines as we have been inclusive since inception, while ensuring each potential team member has the requisite skills, talents, and abilities to be high performing and a valuable contributor.

In my role as executive director, an important area of focus has been on transparency and communication throughout the organization. While I have primary responsibility to MIM's founder and board of trustees, I am also a proponent of sharing timely and relevant information across all levels of our organizational structure. As an example, I started a quarterly "coffee talk" with our volunteer team members (VTMs) shortly after I was appointed executive director. With nearly 500 volunteers helping to advance MIM's mission, it made sense to not only include them in our communications, but also create a forum where they would hear directly from the person leading the organization about MIM's financial health, new projects and initiatives, progress towards institutional goals, and other topics.

This immediately created ownership and buy-in, helping the VTMs to better understand how they were contributing to our objectives and allowed for meaningful conversation around ways they might be able to do more. It also created goodwill. The VTMs thought that if the executive director was willing to take the time to demonstrate the value they bring to the organization by including them in this way, then they must be seen as stakeholders. Indeed, our volunteers are treated as vital constituents to MIM's success and have become integral to our definition of teambuilding.

MIM's board of directors is made up of both local and national high-profile individuals that are committed to the museum's mission and long-term success. Their stewardship and dedication has been critical not only during MIM's launch, but even now, ensuring its founding principles are followed for the foreseeable future. Because MIM's board members have a breadth of skills, leadership talents, and access to important resources, they have helped to propel the museum forward in a short period of time. Working in partnership with the board and MIM's founder, it has been my experience that keeping them apprised of the museum's operations, finances, staffing, and other key areas through quarterly meetings and periodic updates has been very effective. I also take the time to meet with them individually to communicate on a more personal level to ensure their needs and expectations are met. If there is a specific need a board member can assist with, we will reach out directly, which might include fundraising, making an introduction, or attending a special event.

In my estimation, the key to working successfully with MIM's board has been to engage them thoughtfully according to their areas of expertise and abilities. Each board member's experience and knowledge related to marketing, public relations, legal matters, or finance provide invaluable guidance to the museum. Since MIM's founding, we believe that a smaller (between ten and fifteen members), more nimble board would be of greater benefit to our objectives with timelier decision making, follow through, and a shared commitment to mission and brand.

Planning Systems

Every year during the budgeting process, the leadership team looks ahead at the coming year to eighteen months to establish institutional goals and priorities. Less of a formal strategic planning process, this more practical approach to planning leverages a Six Sigma method that guides decision making around specific projects and initiatives.

A great deal of change and evolution has occurred at MIM in the last seven years. A traditional strategic planning process most museums undertake for a longer period would not have served us well and perhaps been counterproductive. Even long-term roadmaps must be flexible and we have found that planning in a shorter, more discrete time frame is increasingly effective as we work to be at the forefront of inevitable change. The methodology currently being used allows us to be more realistic about what is achievable within a twelve- to twenty-four-month period and because we have experimented with various programs that were ultimately short-lived, we were able to make necessary adjustments without significant impact to our core business objectives.

Delivering Mission

MIM was designed by award-winning architect Rich Varda, in collaboration with the Minneapolis and Phoenix firm of RSP Architects. The building's distinctive architecture evokes the topography of the Southwest with materials and patterns that pay homage to the desert landscape, to the rhythms of musical composition, and to the familiar details common to musical instruments from around the world. Indian sandstone is the primary element on the building's dynamic façade. The lobby is light filled and fluid in form. Guests are linked to all the galleries through a spacious main corridor that conjures lyrical forms of music and graceful musical instruments. Likewise, patterns on the floors, walls, and ceilings suggest the geological striations of the Arizona landscape, rhythms of musical composition, and the designs and shapes common to musical instruments.

MIM's collection of nearly 17,000 instruments and artifacts was acquired in the geographic and cultural regions where they are played and have the most cultural relevance. More than 6,500 of these are on exhibit today. Some of the instruments in MIM's collection were, until recently, still being played in their places of origin and were subsequently donated by their makers or the musicians who owned and played them. In fact, guests can see and hear many of them in video clips within each exhibit. The curatorial staff carefully selects instruments for the collection based on their fine construction, makers' reputation, special provenance, or connection to significant performers. While on a musical journey throughout MIM, guests encounter instruments and artifacts in our Geographic Galleries that focus on five major global regions: Africa and the Middle East; Asia and Oceania; Europe; Latin America and the Caribbean; and the United States and Canada.

The facility and collection, as well as state-of-the-art technology, and amenities all combine to deliver on MIM's brand promise and support its mission. We take pride in offering an incomparable, multi-sensory experience in an immersive environment that is bright, cheerful, and welcoming to anyone with an interest in music, world cultures, and musical instruments. While similar museums do exist, they focus primarily on Western instruments. MIM is unique in that it brings together in one place an expansive collection representing and celebrating the music of every country in the world.

Financial Sustainability

Financial sustainability is a reality for every organization, though particularly challenging in the nonprofit sector. The generosity of MIM's Founder has been a necessary lifeline since opening in 2010, though we have successfully reduced his contribution every year thereafter. At the same time, we have established a strong donor base that continues to grow, along with increasing revenues earned from attendance, the museum store, concert attendees, and various programs. The team is also actively involved in finding ways to reduce expenses through utility savings, smarter staffing decisions, and other means.

As a new museum, MIM's current and biggest challenge is perception. The reality is that we rely on the financial support of the community to become sustainable but we are perceived to be an institution without such needs because we have a beautiful new building, the founder made a substantial initial investment, and the team's efforts to effectively message the museum's funding needs have not entirely resonated. So while we are experiencing steady growth, there is still work to be done to overcome this misperception.

Team and volunteer team members, leadership, board and advisory board members alike understand the charge to become self-sustaining and fully operational without founder contributions in just a few short years. While this is no small task, I believe it is achievable and one that requires establishing a culture of philanthropy across the entire organization. With everyone focused on the goal of generating sustained support, MIM will be able to allow future generations to explore and experience the rich diversity of the world's music and musical instruments.

Qualities of Transformative Leaders

Flexibility

In my experience, this has been the most important quality attributable to the success I have realized in my professional career. As they say, change is inevitable and at MIM, flexibility is a way of life. We embrace change and the positive aspects of what it may bring. In fact, one of MIM's core values is to be ever changing, which means our workplace culture relies on each person's ability to adapt to change, both unanticipated and expected. As the leader of the organization, I find it an imperative to be as agile and responsive as possible. Though we have established tried and true programs, processes, and models for success that have led to desired outcomes, there isn't an overreliance on what is predictable, particularly since we are driven to constantly improve. Being part of the making of MIM and now at its helm remains the best lesson in flexibility I can imagine.

Courage

Leadership has always called for courage, a deep level of commitment, and extremely hard work. Today though, the world is more complex, creating challenges that require thoughtful consideration but also decisive action. It takes courageous leadership to confront a particular issue, assess potential implications, and take appropriate measures. Further, stepping into a leadership role itself is an act of courage knowing that one has accepted full responsibility for the stewardship of an organization, whether for-profit or nonprofit. Courage, of course, is not the absence of fear but rather standing firm and remaining consistent in your belief despite the unknown or unfamiliar. It is moving forward in the face of uncertainty and the willingness to lead in what very well may be a moment of truth.

Inspiration

In *Good to Great and the Social Sectors*, Jim Collins remarks, "True leadership only exists if people follow when they have the freedom not to." At MIM, we work to foster an environment of purpose-driven leadership that motivates our teams to deliver on our promise of brand excellence and adding value to the global community. Such leadership requires belief in and ability to articulate a vision for the organization that inspires commitment from each team member. I have found that everyone at MIM wants to contribute meaningfully, have a purpose they understand and relate to, while serving the organization's goals to achieve the best possible outcome. Simply put, leadership must be inspirational because quite often it can define the difference between a good organization and one that is truly exceptional.

My personal and professional development has come from many sources over the years, most recently including an opportunity to attend Harvard Business School for an Executive Leadership certification. Outside of formal institutional settings, I worked with an executive coach when I was initially coming into the role of executive director at MIM, which I found to be extremely beneficial. The practical lessons and tools I was able to immediately apply, coupled with my institutional knowledge, were key to a seamless transition and readiness for the level of responsibility I was assuming. Personal mentors, both in and out of the museum world, have also provided ample guidance and sound advice.

Whatever your path, but most especially in the realm of leadership, I think it's extremely important to continuously learn, stay informed of trends and information relevant to your field, connect with a community of peers, and impart that cumulative knowledge to others as often and as broadly as possible. Having served in the museum field for more than twelve years with plans to continue for many more, I consider it my life's work and what I have always been most passionate about. Whether executive director at MIM or in another capacity elsewhere, if I can meaningfully contribute to this humanitarian endeavor we call museum work, I will have served well.

■   ■   ■

The *Albright-Knox Art Gallery* in Buffalo, New York, is one of the oldest and most distinguished art museums in the United States. Under new leadership the museum has embarked on a transformational reinvention, created a new strategic plan, and launched a major expansion and capital campaign. Director of Advancement Jillian Jones chronicles the changes taking place at the museum with an emphasis on team-based operations and community engagement. She shares her own strategies as a new leader at the museum.

Albright-Knox Art Gallery

Jillian Jones, Director of Advancement

The Albright-Knox is recognized as having one of the world's most important collections of contemporary and modern art. Comprising more than 8,000 works, its holdings are especially rich in post-war American and European art, and art from the 1970s through the end of the twentieth century. Situated at the edge of Buffalo's Frederick Law Olmsted–designed Delaware Park, the museum's main buildings—one Neoclassical and one modern—were designed by celebrated American architects Edward B. Green (1905) and Gordon Bunshaft (1962), respectively. The museum is governed by a thirty-three-member board of directors and managed by a staff of eighty full-time and fifty-three part-time staff, and operates on a budget of over $9,000,000. While it has a substantial endowment, roughly three-quarters is restricted to the acquisition of art. Annually, the museum serves an average of 120,000 visitors on-site, 300,000 on its website, and more than 70,000 across its rapidly growing social media platforms. It also has a Public Art Initiative representing a partnership with the City of Buffalo and the County of Erie. In 2016 it launched a $155,000,000 capital campaign titled "AK360" to expand and refurbish its historic campus and grow its operating endowment. In partnership with the architectural firm OMA/Shohei Shigematsu, the museum will add a wing dedicated to educational initiatives, will expand gallery space and social spaces, and will more deeply integrate the museum's campus with the surrounding Olmsted landscape. With the generous matching gift of Buffalo native Mr. Jeffrey Gundlach in 2016 the museum is well on its way to realizing its ambitious expansion project. The donor will be recognized in renaming the museum as the Albright-Knox Gundlach Art Gallery at the end of the campaign.

The Leadership Team

The museum's leadership team structure was established in 2015 and is intended to promote clarity of mission and purpose, proactive communication, and ultimately, collaboration among division leaders. The structure was designed by Director Dr. Janne Sirén and presents a flexible, cross-functional matrix organized for maximum efficiency. Rather than pulling all members into a lengthy weekly meeting with topics that are not always relevant to all, each month sees three meetings (once per week) that are each devoted to one of the following topics: high-level management issues, program content, or operations. Only relevant staff members are required to attend and decisions are conveyed and discussed in a fourth meeting that includes all division leaders. Dr. Sirén leads all meetings. Mondays are kept sacred for meetings so that staff is free to focus energy elsewhere later in the week.

When division heads participate in the highest levels of strategic organizational management as in this manner, institutional priorities remain clear to everyone. As part of the museum's executive leadership team, I am aware and understanding of my colleagues' distinct interests, which are sometimes at odds with my department's goals. For example, we may have a minimal number of prime evening hours during which we can present public programs. I may hope to present a more popular speaker that can easily garner a sponsor. My colleagues may desire a less well-known speaker that cements a partnership or loan with an overseas institution, but may be difficult to sell as a sponsorship opportunity. Since I have been at the table to hear the conversations that underpin the need for that loan/partnership, I feel more confident knowing when to stand my ground or when to yield to the greater good. In each scenario, I am willing and interested to weigh costs and benefits from a wider variety of angles because I participate in leading the museum as much as I lead my own department. I think that our leadership structure requires all of us to be well rounded and collaborative, ultimately leading to a museum program that has something for everyone.

About the Advancement Team: when I arrived in 2015 I inherited a team of five. I made two immediate changes and one additional hire that effectively redistributed the duties of the department. I added positions in 2016. Positions are responsible for membership, annual giving, advancement services, foundations and government relations, major gifts, events, and facility rentals. The advancement team is organized into three cross-functional groups: one that focuses on annual, unrestricted revenue (membership, annual fund), one focused on restricted and special gifts (Annual Sponsorships or AK360 Capital Campaign), and one focused on the stewardship and events that underpin and bolster all fundraising actions. Each group has a team leader. Some advancement team members find themselves serving on two teams. The idea behind this structure is to build efficiency and relevance into planning, meetings, and events. Further, it is intended to build a second level of leadership into the advancement department where there was previously just one director (me) with eight direct reports. I could not effectively provide proper leadership to each person while also participating in the leadership team and serving as the chief fundraising officer.

Decision Making

In general, the AK senior leadership team focuses on new ideas or endeavors that change the standard operations of the museum or significantly impact revenue, expenses, or the budget. The AK360 Capital Project is one that is widely discussed, but decisions are made at the top level and the board. While the director of the museum exhibits strong leadership, he is also intent upon hearing all sides of a quandary before levying a decision. With a military background, he believes deeply in the wisdom of a team-based approach to operations. A repeated mantra of his that indicates the seriousness with which he approaches his job is "there are no bad teams, only bad leaders," indicating that he takes full responsibility for the museum's well-being.

In the summer of 2016 we launched a new ten-year strategic plan. While a committee of staff members generally wrote the plan, it was formulated with guidance from a consultant and deep engagement and oversight from a committee of the board over a twelve-month period. The staff committee (a cross section of museum staff at various levels across the museum) was engaged in brainstorming and feedback sessions. Staff continue to monitor and drive progress, involving their colleagues in implementation. The plan is divided into four sections:

- Exceptional collections and exhibitions
- Engaging communities
- AK360 (the museum's expansion plan)
- Institutional vigor

The museum has many unique priorities associated with the capital project (AK360). For example, the education department has a new leader as of 2016 who is reorganizing and refreshing the department and its key initiatives. This may seem distinct, except that the new building will have roughly three times the current space devoted to education programming and the changes are being made in anticipation of increasing activity in that realm. Similarly, the notion of "access" and the elimination of barriers to participation in the museum is a key priority, marked by the ambition to designate a space in the new building that is admission free. That space, and its location, is a key driver of the building's design and the related capital campaign. There is one very high priority that I believe exists independent of AK360: increasing diversity throughout our organization.

Engaging our community and doing so in a way that responds to the unique demographics of Western New York is of highest priority. This goal is endorsed and catalyzed by the highest level of leadership (the board), and therefore, it manifests as a thread woven into our daily work. The Albright-Knox serves a community that is extremely diverse, and always has been, welcoming immigrants and refugees throughout its history. But like many museums today the visiting public does not match the diversity of the region.

Without submitting a laundry list of the many programs that we produce in response to our community's needs, I highlight one here. The Public Art Initiative was founded in 2014 to reflect, honor, and expand the diversity of the region's artists, artistic disciplines, and cultural points of view. The goal is to facilitate and elevate the public's awareness of its environment and to expand its engagement, knowledge, and understanding of the arts; it is also to bring awareness to and enhance the many facets of art in the daily lives of county residents and visitors. Led by a Curator of Public Art and two Public Art Project Coordinators, the team fans out across the region, getting to know the neighborhoods, their residents, their elected officials, schools, houses of worship, and libraries. Each project usually connects several different nodes that were previously disconnected and are designed in response to a perceived need in a specific neighborhood. For example, a mural that was painted in a historically Latinx corridor resulted from repeated conversations with residents and the sponsoring business that lamented the lack of a recognizable entryway to the neighborhood. The mural was hosted by a building/business owner, and sponsored by a local business. Community conversations that informed the content of the mural project were facilitated by a group of volunteer community leaders, and community paint days engaged the willing hands of residents from the neighborhood and beyond.

Rapid Prototyping and Flexibility in Planning

I've worked in a very large museum ($40,000,000+ budget) and now a smaller museum ($9,000,000 budget). While I greatly enjoyed the multi-dimensional nature of a large, encyclopedic institution, I embrace the less restrictive nature of the smaller museum where there are less layers of management to work through when making day-to-day decisions. Through this, I have learned a valuable lesson about my personal management style: that I, personally, prefer to lead with flexibility and would rather ask "why not?" than "why?" Why not make next Tuesday a free day because it aligns with one of the mayor's initiatives? Why not throw the membership requirements associated with facility rentals out the window and allow Group X to host an evening here because it engages a new group of collectors? While there are serious boundaries to operating in this manner, such as not overburdening staff with too many events, or putting any art, facilities, or people at risk, we as a museum are more likely to approach our work with a "why not?" attitude than one that is bound by rules and tradition.

We have engaged the notions of rapid prototyping most handily in our AK360 project. From the very beginning we have hosted community meetings that invited the public to comment on when, why, and where we should institute a capital project. Public meetings engaged the community in this journey: (1) we asked them to learn and comment on WHY we need a new building (over 400 people participated), (2) we asked them to meet the architect and landscape architect, who shared their aspirations for a renewed campus, and (3) we asked them to actually place blocks that represent future architectural volumes on maps of campus to show us how they might construct a new facility. This engagement with the public will continue in future phases of the capital project. We also apply this tactic with respect to the Public Art Initiative. Each new project invites a block club or congregation to provide feedback on a planned project. The feedback is taken very seriously and integrated into the final product.

Diversity of Board and Staff

Unfortunately, only 15 percent of the museum's staff identify with an EEO code other than "white," with .8 percent identifying a disability. Further, of thirty-three active board of directors members, only two represent a minority group. However, the desire to change this is strong and the strategic plan reflects that desire under its "Institutional Vigor" platform, which lays out plans for diversifying our staff and audience. Also, in early 2017 the Governance Committee of the board conducted a self-assessment to identify the most critical gaps in its membership and to construct a plan for recruitment. We address these issues as honestly as possible, and realize this is an issue plaguing the museum sector writ large. Our HR practices seek as large a pool as possible for each open position and we talk about our struggles in identifying that diverse pool at the highest levels of management. Hiring managers are expected to actively recruit potential candidates, not just wait for candidates to find the position. Further, we regularly identify gift and granting opportunities that would help diversify our staff. In this way, the Advancement team often takes a leadership role in building diversity into our staff. In 2016 we were awarded a one-year grant by New York state to hire a Curatorial Fellow for Diversity, available only to historically underrepresented candidates.

Thoughts on Leadership

In general, my leadership philosophy is the following: Step 1—hire talented people and charge them to do their best work. Step 2—remove the obstacles that impede their success. I believe that my job as a manager is to empower my staff. This notion of *empowerment* breeds proactivity. This arrangement requires implicit *trust*; my employees must know that I always have their back. This means that I will back up their decisions publically and that I will *advocate for their success* (personally and professionally) up the chain and in the public realm. This is critically important for an externally facing department like Advancement. I am able to do this successfully because I feel this sense of trust and empowerment from the person to whom I report (the director).

Leadership also requires *humility*. Sometimes I think our most challenging impediment to success is our self, our own ego. "Getting out of my own way" by asking how my approach to solving a problem may be fueled by a desire for recognition, or to save face, requires self-awareness and the knowledge that we cannot be all things to all people. This has been the most difficult lesson to learn as a relatively young leader (I was thirty-three at the time that I stepped into my director of advancement role), and I still struggle with it, particularly as a new mother. This struggle—the desire to excel at all tasks on multiple levels simultaneously, to essentially perform "perfectly"—has arisen in many a conversation with other women, regardless of how many hats they wear.

Finally, *confidence* has been a leadership quality that I've had to cultivate. This may not mean that I feel total conviction that I've made the right decision, but if that decision/strategy/direction is relayed to others with confidence and no indication of ambivalence, they will feel a sense of clarity about their role in the matter at hand, contributing further to notions of productivity and empowerment. When I was first considering my current role, I remember feelings of intimidation, thinking that it would be an ambitious leap for someone my age. But I also remember reading the job description and thinking, "I can do this job." From that moment, I proceeded with confidence that this was the right path forward. It doesn't mean that I never second-guessed myself. It just means that I *never let anyone else know* I was second-guessing myself, so no one has ever (to my knowledge) second-guessed me. I say all of that with a grain of salt. Leaders are human. Humans are fragile, and therefore vulnerable. I think we adapt by building an excellent support network. I have several colleagues who are also close friends. We allow each other to be human from time to time and we make sure that we take care of one another.

I also think that there is a time for "innovative" and "new," but that always reinventing the wheel in your work leads to exhaustion within your team. Innovation is critical for adaptability, but so is predictability. I (and by default, my team) spent our first two years together building a new team, new systems, new relationships, and so on. Everything—even our basic systems—was new and when a wrench was thrown in the system that required us to adapt, we had a hard time doing so because there was nothing solid to fall back on. Now, two years into a more or less reliable annual calendar and a steady working rhythm, we have space to embrace whatever surprise is coming our way. We have the safety net that gives us freedom to adapt. Therefore, adaptability requires some level of stability, even though it may take time to find that solid ground.

※　※　※

The *Virginia Historical Society* case study features the work of a new director at a well-established museum. Jamie O. Bosket took over leadership of the museum in the spring of 2017 and like many new directors launched a strategic planning effort and reorganization. His work is characteristic of an adaptive and focused approach to leading change. Communication is a major emphasis in his transformational work. This profile is based on an interview with the author.

Virginia Historical Society

Jamie O. Bosket, President and CEO

Founded in 1831, the Virginia Historical Society (VHS) is the oldest cultural organization in the Commonwealth of Virginia, and one of the oldest and most distinguished history organizations in the nation. Located in the Museum District of Richmond, Virginia, the VHS houses its collection of nearly 9,000,000 items and serves as the state history museum with permanent and special exhibitions as well as a vibrant portfolio of public programs. The VHS is a private, nonprofit organization. It is governed by a board of trustees of nearly 30 people, selected from across the Commonwealth. The current paid staff is comprised of nearly 100 people, and a volunteer corps of about 40 people. The museum operates with an annual budget of approximately $7,000,000. The headquarters museum is nearly 250,000 square feet, and they maintain an additional historic property on the James River called Virginia House.

The Challenge of a New Leader

Jamie Bosket assumed the role of president and CEO in early 2017. Prior to this post he was vice president for Guest Experience at George Washington's Mount Vernon. Bosket had a series of increasingly responsible positions at Mount Vernon. His decade there provided opportunity to hone skills in people management and collaboration. Moving to VHS at the age of 33 made Bosket one of the youngest museum directors in the country. Given the long and distinguished history of the museum Bosket was excited to take on a new chapter for the organization. Like all museums the VHS has gone through various phases of the organizational life cycle. In the past two decades the museum completed a period of major expansion and growth, primarily under the leadership of Charles Bryan Jr. Following on the tenure of a highly regarded and successful leader is always daunting and Bosket takes that role seriously. His intention to build on that success is important. The work he is undertaking for the VHS is to "pivot to a far more public-engaging organization." Drawing on the best encyclopedic collection on the history of Virginia, VHS will succeed through telling a remarkable and relevant story. His vision is to create a more "vibrant, inclusive, people-centric" organization.

On Strategic Planning and New Directions

One of the first steps toward this new vision involved a comprehensive listening tour of staff, board, peers, and other stakeholders. Over a period of several months Bosket met with every staff member in the organization and visited each board member, and with each session encouraged candid reflections and aspirations. This allowed him to quickly identify a number of important trending topics and to get a better understanding of personalities and skillsets. Although VHS is an older and more conservative cultural organization he was pleased to encounter enthusiasm and good ideas everywhere he went. He believes strongly in the power of listening to set a new standard for the organization. As ideas congealed and he gained traction on his vision for embracing a larger and more inclusive audience, he determined to mark the occasion with a meaningful large-scale public program. On July 4, 2017, the museum held its first citizenship ceremony, which provided a way to showcase the diversity of the city and state, and signal to the community that their story will be included in the museum's programs. It proved to be highly successful and was the VHS's busiest day in more than a decade. It was a great short-term win to energize the staff and jump-start momentum.

The museum plans to roll out a new five-year plan and institutional brand in early 2018 that will prominently feature public engagement. In advance of this they will conduct community conversations about their perceptions and desires for the museum. Additionally, Bosket has forged revitalized partnerships with both the state Science and Art museums and the many other likeminded organizations in the region.

Leading Change

To encourage staff to embrace the idea of working more closely with visitors and the community, Bosket has taken initial steps to prototype new programs, and to gently push the staff outside their comfort zone. The first was the July 4 citizenship event. Another was to host a craft beer festival. Brewers were invited to work with recipes from the museum archives. Fortunately this was a popular event. Bosket is encouraging the staff to be more nimble, embrace success, and be okay with an occasional failure. He noted that to be fully relevant, you must be willing to accept smart risk.

As with many new leaders, strategic planning and change are important. Bosket is a people person and consistently in tune with the needs of his staff. He certainly understands that the challenge for staff to embrace change is not easy. During one of his all-staff town hall sessions, he shared a quote with the staff that he had recently read: "a ship in harbor is safe, but that is not what ships are built for." He went on to note that it may be easier to deflect change and risk, but a collection and story of the magnitude of the VHS's deserves more. The nearly two centuries of collecting, preserving, and research must be allowed their full value through greater exposure and impact.

Like many new leaders Bosket needed to reinforce the change process through a major reorganization. New organizational units, staff assignments, and new bosses were appointed, including a new vice president post to serve as advocate for audiences. In follow-up to the reorganization Bosket has taken steps to put a spotlight on staff. He has hired the museum's first human resource manager, and implemented mandatory training in new ways of doing business. In staffing, like most museums, there is aspiration to become more diverse. This is particularly important as the museum engages new audiences and focuses on more public facing activities.

Further efforts to implement change involve working with a seasoned trainer on leadership skills, and clarifying roles and responsibilities. This initiative is a critical part of reorganizing the staff into new units and setting new overarching priorities. All efforts to define roles and responsibilities will be widely shared with staff. Other training will include short workshops for cross sections of staff to learn more about approaches to creativity and collaboration.

Communications

Bosket believes in sharing information widely. He has launched a program to "balance out" the conversations between all levels of the organization. Every month he shares a substantial report on operations with the board, something very different from what they have received before. He always gathers data from the staff and produces a metrics dashboard in the report. Then, the same report that goes to the board is shared with all staff. This serves to include the board in the conversations about the new direction of the museum and to show staff how their successes are shared with the board. Seeing trust as a fundamental concern of leading change, he shares with all staff the minutes of weekly senior team meetings and the briefing materials provided to the board. As a result he is experiencing more positive dialogue with the staff. This is clearly a best practice in the field of museum leadership.

Personally Bosket notes that "you can't fully anticipate what to expect" in taking on a new position, particularly as a first-time CEO.

In fact he referenced the debate over the fate of Civil War monuments in the city and throughout the state. These external events can't be predicted but need to be addressed. Building a strong staff and external partnerships, and solidifying the institution's identity and priorities, are critical steps to sustaining the organization through changing times. Overall Bosket is thrilled to be able to take on the challenge of leading a change effort saying "there is nothing more rewarding than making positive and impactful change at a place that matters!!"

Jamie O. Bosket is president and CEO of the Virginia Historical Society. Prior to this he worked at George Washington's Mt. Vernon, where he rose to vice president for Guest Experience. His career began in upstate New York where he worked at the Genesee Country Village and Museum and the Corning-Painted Post Historical Society. He has degrees in history and museum studies and has been nationally recognized as an emerging leader in the cultural sector.[3]

The *Smithsonian Institution* is the world's largest museum and research complex. With over nineteen museums and research units and 6,500 staff the daunting challenge of implementing a strategic plan in 2010 presented a unique opportunity for collaboration. Under the leadership of Dr. Wayne Clough (secretary from 2008 to 2015) the institution launched the Grand Challenges program. The goal was to move from silos to teams and to showcase this as a best practice in organizational design and development. This case study was written by two principal leaders of that initiative, Michelle Delaney and Elizabeth Kirby.

Convening Teams of Scholars: How the Smithsonian Institution Fostered Cross-Disciplinary Collaboration

Michelle Delaney and Elizabeth Kirby

The MacArthur Foundation's 100&Change program that aims to solve a critical problem facing humanity, the Giant Magellan Telescope that promises to revolutionize our view and understanding of the universe, and Digging into Data examining how large-scale computational techniques can be used to answer questions in the

humanities and social sciences—these programs embody the exciting potential of twenty-first-century research: big and collaborative.
In a world where problems are too complex for any one branch of
knowledge to solve alone, answers are found where disciplines intersect. How do we provide our scholars with the resources and skills to
excel in these important efforts? The Smithsonian Grand Challenges
Consortia was an institution-wide initiative that recognized the solutions to society's biggest issues would come from those who would
work together. The consortia galvanized the formation of interdisciplinary research teams and provided a range of enabling assistance to
allow the scholars to convene. Consortia support was described once
as the "match that lit the fuse, if you will, actually letting us do the
work." This is the story of how a 170-year-old institution embarked
on a great experiment.

Museum Context

The curious history of the Smithsonian begins in Europe, with the
birth in 1765 of James Macie Smithson. As a young man he traveled
across England, Scotland, and Europe, meeting some of the most
important men of his era. Considering the time of the Enlightenment
in Europe, Smithson's thirst for knowledge, innovation, and collecting is comparable to many of his contemporaries. When he died in
1829, leaders in the United States were unaware of the future impact
this Englishman, who never visited the country, would make on the
history of science, art, history, and culture in America. His will stipu-
lated that, if his heirs should decease prematurely, his estate should be
transferred to the United States for the establishment of the "Smithsonian Institution" with the mission of the *increase and diffusion of
knowledge among men.*"

Congress created the Smithsonian Institution as a federal establishment, not part of the three branches of government, managed by a
self-perpetuating board of regents. The board's first act was to build a
home for the Institution, a Norman Castle designed by architect James
Renwick Jr., located on the National Mall in Washington, DC. The
regents also selected Joseph Henry, one of the most prominent scientists in the nation, an experimental physicist from the College of New
Jersey (Princeton), as the first secretary of the Smithsonian. Henry's

focus for the Institution would remain on science research, while the regents envisioned broader potential for the Smithsonian.

The growth and expansion of the Smithsonian since the days of Henry in the Castle reflect the strategic leadership of each of the thirteen secretaries, their expectations and their priorities. Today, the Smithsonian Institution has become one of the world's largest museum, education, and research complexes. It includes nineteen museums and galleries, twenty libraries, the National Zoo, and numerous research centers, such as the Smithsonian Astrophysics Observatory, the Smithsonian Tropical Research Institute, and the Smithsonian Environmental Research Center. It has an annual budget of just over $1 billion, 6,500 employees, and 6,300 volunteers. Its federal appropriation accounts for 62 percent of the Institution's funding. The Smithsonian generates additional funding from private contributions and business revenues. It is managed by a board of regents working with a secretary who oversees the organization. The Castle continues to serve as the seat of central leadership.

The Smithsonian mission remains: *The increase and diffusion of knowledge.* This simple mission statement grounded the strategic plan, *Inspiring Generations through Knowledge and Discovery 2010–2015,* centering the Institution around four Grand Challenges, each an institutional strength.

Strategic Planning and the Change Effort

For the Smithsonian, the nineteenth century was defined by collections growth and the twentieth century by the founding of discrete museums and centers, each developing deep layers of scholarship within their specialized fields. In the twenty-first century, the Smithsonian turned to integrating the various parts of the Institution. Whether the opportunity was education or bridging cultural gaps, whether the challenge was global warming or species extinction, the Smithsonian offered a breadth of resources and depth of expertise. To realize its true potential, leadership aimed to transform the Institution, connecting its collections and the intellectual capital of its scholars across disciplines in ways that increased its value to society. Driven by the strategic plan, the Institution brought in a new era, calling for broadened access, revitalized education, strengthened collections, and bold new ways of thinking that offered different ways of working. Developed by more than 1,000 staff, the plan signaled an important shift in emphasis, addressing the need to cross internal and external boundaries while focusing work around the four Grand Challenges that served as the organizational framework. It offered a comprehensive vision that was wide enough to incorporate different areas of intellectual curiosity and creativity.

- *Unlocking the Mysteries of the Universe:* The Smithsonian had played a leading role in understanding the fundamental nature of the universe, dark matter, galaxy formation, and extreme explosive phenomena in the universe. Now it would extend the focus to apply the integrative research of its scientists to today's big questions regarding the origin and evolution of the earth, planets, stars, galaxies, and the universe, yielding tremendous impact through the collaborative energy of scientists, scholars, and cultural experts.
- *Understanding and Sustaining a Biodiverse Planet:* Historically, the Smithsonian studied species in a range of ecosystems with the goal of enhancing knowledge of biodiversity and its role in the healthy functioning of ecosystems for a sustainable planet. It would now broker increased interdisciplinary research and harness its Institutional power to expand its work and find innovative approaches to cataloging problems that stem from biodiversity loss, ecosystem degradation, and climate change.
- *Valuing World Cultures:* Throughout its history the Smithsonian had contributed greatly to the world's knowledge, understanding, and respect for the evolution of humanity and the diversity of the world's cultures. It would now expand its museum and research centers' cross-cultural scholarship, exhibitions, and programming. The collections, from the ancient to the contemporary, would be used as the basis to fully represent and understand the breadth of cultural creativity and diversity in our world.
- *Understanding the American Experience:* The Smithsonian advanced and synthesized knowledge that contributed to understanding the American experience—its history, arts, and culture and the sciences. Facing forward, the Smithsonian would foster a pan-institutional approach that encouraged interdisciplinary

project teams to document the historic and contemporary accomplishments and creativity of the American people.

Originally, the idea was to create four centers, one around each challenge. As the strategic planning process evolved, leadership noticed that when people began talking about how the centers could collaborate, sparks flew. Internal studies done by the Smithsonian examining work that involved the nexus of history, art, culture, and science noted that all complex problems facing the world such as poverty, climate change, loss of cultural and biodiversity, and geopolitical tensions required multidisciplinary solution finding. In 2010, the Smithsonian formed the Grand Challenges Consortia to serve as the catalyst that would bring scholars together, drawing from every field to develop new knowledge, advance research, and provide core content to inform exhibition, curricula, and public programs. The consortia would be the means for realizing the strategic plan and the potential of the Institution.

The Model

In considering models, the Smithsonian looked at the new ways organizations large and small were finding to connect both people and data so they could support problem solving from multiple perspectives. At the federal level, the National Science Foundation and the National Institutes of Health, had designed programs to advance cross-disciplinary, integrated scholarly efforts. Academia also offered successful models for developing interdisciplinary research and education. These included leaders with joint appointments that spanned traditional academic units to bring about culture change. Work processes that organized scholars to solve problems outside established hierarchies supported a broadened view of age-old, scholarly challenges. The corporate sector, with its focus on teams and rapid response to customer needs, also served as an example. The Grand Challenges Consortia would also help ensure that the Institution continued to recruit and retain the best and the brightest scholars, curators, scientists, and educators, since many professionals seek environments that foster interdisciplinary work.

There were certainly risks and challenges associated with the development of the consortia, especially whether units would utilize it and support it. The researchers the consortia hoped to attract would need to see acceptance by their directors. To develop buy-in, the unit directors were invited to contribute as formal and informal advisors, functioning as executive committee members for the consortium. They also engaged in a range of other activities, including annual briefings, sign-offs on the proposals submitted to the consortia, and visibility for their scholars through project showcase events. Research was performed and exhibitions developed by a large measure, within the units. The goal was to have the unit directors view the consortia as conduits of new contributions to intellectual discourse occurring across the institution, without taking the focus from the work of the units themselves. The scholars also needed to see opportunities that would allow them to achieve their intellectual goals. With incentives like opportunities for convening colleagues around mutual areas of interest, seed funds to experiment with new ideas, as well as human resources to help with concept development and pursuit of external funding, the consortia found scholars eager to get involved.

The Strategic Goal: Strengthening Interdisciplinary Efforts

Collectively and individually, the four consortia would incubate, develop, and launch collaborations across the Smithsonian. They would also serve as an important force for cross-institutional activity. To lead the shift from more unit-driven to cross-institutional activity, the consortia would help researchers achieve both an internal and external goal. First, its projects would address one or more of the Grand Challenges through an interdisciplinary, multi-unit approach that would capitalize on the breadth of intellectual talent within the Institution. Second, the projects would amplify the Smithsonian's leadership in addressing the Grand Challenges, nationally and globally, by enhancing externally funded research, thereby increasing the public's awareness of related issues. It would also develop critical partnerships with outside organizations that would complement Smithsonian expertise and reach new audiences. These efforts would culminate in the development of important programs that addressed critical issues facing the world.

The Structure and Staffing

The Bill and Melinda Gates Foundation provided grant funding to accelerate interdisciplinary research at the Smithsonian. At the center of the project was the formation of four consortia. Each consortium was led by a prominent Smithsonian scholar who showed leadership in developing collaborations in their own field and was now charged with coalescing interest groups from across the institution. Housed together in the Smithsonian Castle, the consortia office suite earned the affectionate nickname, "the bullpen." The consortia directors' proximity to each other provided opportunities to discuss mutual areas of interest and share strategies for working across the institution. Situated near the offices of the Under Secretary for Science and the Under Secretary for History, Art, and Culture to whom consortia directors reported, this location also allowed them to communicate regularly with the Secretary of the Smithsonian and other cabinet level members of the central administration. This placement also made a significant statement about the consortia as an institution-wide resource. Consortia directors were supported by three staff members who provided technical assistance to ensure that researchers had comprehensive help with their projects.

Grants Development Specialist—experienced in proposal development and award administration, who worked with teams of scholars on developing concepts for external funding and partnerships, alerted them to potential opportunities, and worked with teams of Smithsonian scholars to assemble large, complex proposals.

Financial Manager—experienced in financial administration at the Institution and who worked with the finances of the seed grant program and assisted researchers with developing financial arrangements across units, each of which operated with their own administrative cultures.

Administrative Assistant—responsible for proving administrative support to keep teams moving forward, which included scheduling and supporting regular meetings with project teams, and planning for conferences, symposia, and other events.

To jump-start its engagement with the institution the consortia relied on multiple strategies, such as bottom up idea fairs and top down working groups to foster new projects and relationships.

Idea fairs brought together scholars from across the institution to explore and develop preliminary ideas for projects in a collegial setting. The first Smithsonian Idea Fair took place in March 2010, and focused on projects related to the consortium for *Understanding the American Experience*. Proposals were submitted for consideration at the Fair including projects for photography, immigration, and music. These topics built on current activities and staff expertise and leveraged collections and assets. Proposal ideas were interdisciplinary and inter-unit, and relevant to societal problems or innovation in particular fields. Each one identified a research question or agenda and put forth concepts for public education programs and outreach.

Working groups were commissioned by central leadership to develop proposals in areas of research that were clear targets for consortia activities, based on Grand Challenges content, scholarly expertise, and potential for significant impact. Initially, three working groups formed: one on climate change and carbon sequestration, one on computational modeling, and a third on cultural property. These groups explored what was already being done across the Smithsonian—where core strengths lay, where there were weaknesses and how to address them—in order to develop blueprints for possible directions for consortia projects.

To seed entrepreneurial activities, consortia grants were awarded at two different levels. Level One grants provided seed money to develop groups around promising concepts. Level Two grants were larger and aimed at maturing groups poised to confront relevant issues and prepared to secure external funding. Successful proposals at the Level One stage provided the time and incentive for individuals with common interests to meet and crystallize ideas for major interdisciplinary projects. Level Two funding allowed interdisciplinary teams to conduct preliminary experiments, write position papers, or produce other evidence of scholarly advancement deemed essential for external competition. Successful proposals at Level Two provided groups with the resources they needed to establish themselves as credible competitors for external funding, allowing for presentation of preliminary success in a field or demonstrating capacity.

In promoting the consortia to institution stakeholders, the emphasis was on providing a turbo boost of service that would allow teams of researchers to reach the next level of the project, rather than adding a new layer of bureaucracy. To keep the consortia management nimble, the institution relied as much as possible on the infrastructure already in place in units across the institution. This arrangement also confirmed the commitment of the unit to the project and ensured that unit support would continue as interdisciplinary activity increased. While the consortia office helped with concepts and proposal development, the units managed grants once awarded.

In terms of goals and outcomes for the consortia, the activities were designed to establish intellectual focus and position the Institution for the future by uniting efforts to develop leadership programs of global significance. Directors of museums and research centers came to view the consortia as an asset that benefited their own units by promoting cross-unit collaborations and providing resources. Conceived as a temporary organization, the expectation was that each consortium would develop at least one highly visible signature program that secured major external grant funding, led to a new exhibition or exhibition plan, and/or resulted in seminal research and publications in the field. Through these efforts the Smithsonian would gain greater visibility for its scholarship and further validate the importance of the Grand Challenges in the public sector.

An Example Project: Civil War 150

The *Civil War 150* project is an excellent example of how consortia support worked and brought the assets of the Institution to serve a scholarly team. The 150th anniversary of the Civil War, an important occasion marked by many museums, was also part of Smithsonian History. When the American Civil War erupted in 1861, Secretary Henry pulled down the American Flag and kept the Smithsonian neutral, continuing daily operations and national expeditions as possible. Several of his board of regents members were Southerners, including his close friend Jefferson Davis. Two hundred rounds of ammunition were sent to the front steps of the Castle for protection, but Henry refused to allow troops to move into the Castle. President Lincoln looked to Henry as a science and technology advisor. Tests for signals were sent from the towers of the Smithsonian to the White House, and the first experiments with telegraph signals from balloons to the ground for reconnaissance were tested from the current site of the National Air and Space Museum on the Mall. How the Institution would come together around a unified Civil War project and deal with difficult history was important.

It is a particularly good example because it is transferable to a variety of institutions that may want to view a particular project from multiple perspectives and it can be scaled for two, twenty, or more researchers engaged in a similar effort. The process also lends itself to a project conducted with multiple institutions. The *Civil War 150* brought researchers from around the institution together to strategize around a Smithsonian-wide effort to commemorate the 150th anniversary of the Civil War. One of its most enduring projects was a book titled *Smithsonian Civil War: Inside the National Collection*. It had forty-six authors, an editorial committee of twelve, and sixty staff working on objects and illustrations of the book that examined the Civil War through an interdisciplinary perspective.

Implementation success: Development of a process for selecting a project and the participants that created institutional buy-in for the project and how it was fostered.

A Civil War team had initially developed but never progressed to the formal organization stage because agreement on the staff time, contributions, and goals of the project had not been secured. In 2011, the consortium director initiated convening of more than fifty staff to discuss how to proceed with important 150th commemorations, and pull Smithsonian efforts together with funding options for exhibitions, publications, and programs. One scholar assessed the consortia assistance as, "The Consortia challenged us to think about how to broaden our understanding of the Smithsonian's Civil War collections, the Director of the Consortium for Understanding the American Experience, convened a group of people from across the Smithsonian that were all working on Civil War projects but didn't necessarily know one another, giving us the opportunity to build new partnerships and work cooperatively across the Institution."

An important part of this process was the emergence of team co-leaders, from two different museums, who had never met prior to this activity. They worked with the consortium director to implement the project and obtain concurrence on project implementation from unit management. Each leader championed project components based on their areas of expertise. The consortium director served as content integrator, when needed, and resolved administrative and logistical issues, leaving the leaders free to focus on the intellectual aspects. The director also contacted professional organizations about the project resulting in Smithsonian participation in the National Council on Public History's Civil War Workshop, giving the team an outside perspective from the beginning of the project.

Implementation success: The development of research-driven teams that led in the production of new knowledge, creation of innovative publications and media, and the enhancement of Smithsonian research infrastructure.

The consortia directors organized, facilitated, and negotiated within the Institution for and with the team in framing the project scope and the institutional commitment to realize the project. The directors led the initial meetings to ensure that all units had an equal voice and that discussions focused on the work product. The consortia also provided funding for an internal project coordinator. The co-leaders mobilized the team efforts with two external experts who provided outside perspective on the project potential. The external experts participated in discussions with Smithsonian scholars to define the overall research plan and articulate discrete proposals. They also helped choose outside organizations who would participate as resource organizations for the project. The consortia assisted in finding additional potential external partners, including university and external organizations with digital humanities experience to provide advice on website development and presentation of research content via other media.

Implementation success: Creation and management of the organizational framework that facilitated the model's success.

The organizational framework included stakeholders from all over the Smithsonian. Working together were the excellent and cooperative project leads, the scholar group who authored the articles in the book, the consortia team supporting overall organization and external funding assistance, and senior leadership who made the project visible through their endorsement. The consortium director negotiated a royalty agreement for the book that provided modest funding for new efforts. Collaborators included staff from National Museum of American History, Smithsonian American Art Museum, National Portrait Gallery, National Air and Space Museum, National Museum of African-American History and Culture, Cooper-Hewitt Smithsonian Design Museum, National Museum of Natural History, Smithsonian Anacostia Community Museum, and the Smithsonian Institution Archives and Libraries. The group also received a Secretary's Collaborative Team award providing internal recognition of their work.

Outcomes and Products of the Project

The project developed a comprehensive book with thirteen units participating and provided assistance to help Smithsonian authors with research and writing. As a result of the extensive institutional participation by scholars, the consortium director encouraged many outreach and marketing departments of different Smithsonian units to engage in rare joint promotion and advertising, which extended the reach of the project to include book ads in the *Washington Post* and *New York Times*. There was also an effect on the collections and how they were used in the project. Collections that had been separated—the National Museum of American History and the National Portrait Gallery John Brown collections—were brought together in a new context and scholars learned of important objects, collections, and connections previously unknown to them.

Consortia support allowed for common resources such as a basic Smithsonian Civil War website and social media accounts on Twitter and Facebook managed by individual units and new media offices as volunteers for a cohesive Smithsonian presence online and for social media. Exhibitions that were already in the works at the National Portrait Gallery, Smithsonian American Art Museum, and the Anacostia Community Museum were marketed together through new efforts by central Smithsonian external affairs. Outreach efforts to external organizations brought attention to the project through articles and image inclusion in the 150th anniversary issue of *The Atlantic*; a joint exhibition in the Castle between the Civil War Trust and the Smithsonian, and web presence for the exhibition objects; and the hosting of the Civil War Trust Summer Teacher Institute for several days.

How the Smithsonian Is Using What Was Learned

The development and format of the Civil War 150 book is being used as a template for a new *Women's History Initiative* with an expected publication release in 2019. Through the convening process, the Institution has been able to increase Smithsonian scholar participation in the book design and the research on the collections that will ensure an engaging and comprehensive publication. The recognized success of the Civil War book development process that worked across units to recruit many authors has encouraged senior management to support this new project. Royalties raised are supporting next stage work, and collaboration on this new publication.

Consortia: Successes and Recommendations

The consortia catalyzed change throughout the organization through interdisciplinary program development, enhanced external funding, and greater public recognition of Smithsonian research. From the 165 seed grants and 300 scholars who received funding, there are nine primary programs that have emerged as Smithsonian-wide priorities with the potential to improve life in our time and for the generations to come. The subjects cover the span of the arts and science, ranging from Conservation to Marine Science, to Cultural Heritage Recovery and Preservation. These programs currently reside in different unit homes and retain their interdisciplinary character through continued team activities. Although the consortia sun set in May 2016 and its staff have moved to the Office of the Provost and Under Secretary for Museums and Research, scholars from around the Institution still use the convening techniques to explore new areas of common interest. Program leaders are self-directed with their museum or research unit supporting administration of projects, and regular consultation with collaborating units and the Office of the Provost to foster external partnership development and overall growth and capacity of the programs.

The lessons of the consortia in determining a program that can successfully scale can be applied to other contexts. In reviewing the programs that went forward as institutional priorities, consideration was given to the following questions:

1. What is the intellectual framework underlying the program, and how will this framework be enhanced in the next stage of development?
2. What has been the strategy for securing external support for the program in the past, what success has been achieved, and what is the prognosis for future support to allow the program to reach its desired capacity for national and international impact?
3. Is it appropriate for the program to be located in a particular unit for sustained administrative support? Which unit would best suit the needs of the program and enhance its intellectual activities?
4. What will success look like for this program in the next several years, and further into the future? What modifications do we need to make to the implementation plans for the program, partnerships, staffing, and budget based on the outcomes of this decision.

With regard to transferable components, almost all organizations have seed funding or internal grant programs. Implementing accompanying intellectual and technical assistance such as that provided by the consortia staff can be done for a defined time period with staff time and expertise from existing resources. This kind of team participation has the additional benefit of providing professional development for staff. Also helpful to our researchers was the guidance provided by the four consortia directors during the concept development period. The consortia directors were long-term employees of the Institution who had strong records of scholarly achievement. They served as intellectual peers and helped researchers navigate a complex administrative organization when doing work that transcended units.

What are the transferable lessons from consortia support?

1. Build on the familiar internal/seed grant model and add accompanying support services, ranging from a scholarly director to project enabling administrative assistance, to increase impact.
2. Encourage buy-in from management through support for unit priorities as outlined in proposals from their scholars. A seed grant application question, for example, could ask how the project fits in with the future plans of the unit.

3. Provide internal and external recognition for new efforts undertaken by scholars, ranging from public presentations of seed grant projects to congratulatory notes from central leadership.
4. Infuse the projects with fresh perspectives on how external funding and outreach events can advance their work. Discussion of these topics during the project development phase inspired scholars to include them in project timelines.
5. Make it clear that the primary goal of the assistance is research development. The fact that the consortia staffing structure did not grow and that units received credit for the projects made it clear that no new bureaucratic infrastructure was being created.
6. Use the effort to develop materials that can offer a roadmap for institutionalizing programs and the processes for organization-wide convening.

Beyond its primary goal of assisting researchers, what enhancements could have been added to the consortia's work?

1. Most of the consortia outreach beyond the seed grants funding was through live and webcast events that showcased the scholars and their work. The consortia developed a website in year three after there was sufficient seed grant content to populate it. Putting up the website earlier to communicate with the institution at large would have been helpful.
2. With more time, the consortia might have developed more materials sharing the administrative lessons learned from working across a large organization.

The primary function of the consortia was to bring researchers together and provide them with the tools to excel. The consortia's transition involved institutionalizing the programs created by the scholar teams. The provost's office led a review of each program and then worked with unit directors and program leadership to help create innovative management agreements that provided one administrative home and codified interdisciplinary participation for future program development, which includes on-going report-ins to the provost. Consortia staff joined the provost's office and continues to provide guidance to the existing programs and to emerging groups of scholars using the techniques developed by the consortia to explore new inter-disciplinary programs.

Under new central leadership, the Under Secretary for History, Art, and Culture and the Under Secretary for Science merged to become the Office of the Provost and Under Secretary for Museums and Research in 2015. This new structure allows for administrative cooperation that mirrors the interdisciplinary work of the scholars. Over the long term, the projects developed by Smithsonian researchers with consortia assistance will drive scholarship, increase the resources available to our nation's primary and secondary schools, spark dynamic exhibitions, and grow new sources of revenue for the Smithsonian. Most of all, they will help in the effort to transform a venerable Institution for a new century, ensuring its relevance for generations to come.

Selected Bibliography

Ewing, Heather. *The Lost World of James Smithson*. New York: Bloomsbury, 2007.

Smithsonian Civil War: Inside the National Collection. Washington, DC: Smithsonian Books, 2013.

Smithsonian Grand Challenges Consortia office correspondence and grant files, 2010–2016, Office of the Provost/Under Secretary for Museums and Research, Smithsonian Institution. http://consortia.si.edu/

Smithsonian Institution. https://www.si.edu/about.

Smithsonian Institution Annual Reports. http://library.si.edu/digital-library/book/annual-report-board-regents-smithsonian-institution.

Smithsonian Institution Annual Reports, 2004–2016. https://www.si.edu/about/annual-report

Smithsonian Institution Archives. https://siarchives.si.edu/history/james-smithson.

Smithsonian Institution Strategic Plan, 2010–2015. https://www.si.edu/Content/Pdf/About/SI_Strategic_Plan_2010-2015.pdf.

■ ■ ■

Concluding Thoughts

These case studies are an excellent compendium of details associated with leadership and organizational change. As we have examined in the earlier chapters of this book, the challenges for museums are enormous and implementing change takes numerous skills, passion, opportunity, and courage. The many individuals highlighted in these case studies and throughout the text are to be commended for their dedication and creativity. Each has been very much affected by the presence of strong boards and others who have come before them in advancing the mission of their museums. Clearly there is no single solution but many ways to approach the leadership challenge as these case studies reveal. Hopefully these stories will spark more innovation in the field and assure a resilient and sustainable future for museums.

Discussion Questions

1. Considering the case studies above, which museums are employing innovative practices as outlined in chapter 6?
2. How would these museums benefit from following John Kotter's eight steps for organizational change?
3. Which leaders are the most adaptive in responding to community engagement goals?
4. Are there models of staff development and inclusion in these case studies that could be replicated at your museum?

Notes

1. Author phone interview with Elizabeth Pierce, May 23, 2017.
2. Author personal interview with Jack Rasmussen, November 22, 2016.
3. Author phone interview with Jamie O. Bosket, August 25, 2017.

Appendix A

PERSONALITY ASSESSMENTS AND LEARNING STYLES

The links below provide a free online personality assessment tool for individuals. There are many options for this type of analysis including the Myers Briggs Type Indicator, DISC, and Four Frames. The value of these assessments is in self-awareness in regard to how one processes information, reacts to others, and makes decisions. Preferences are never completely cut and dried, but provide a glimpse into the diversity of the workplace. In general, there are styles that favor the big picture: creativity and fast decisions (entrepreneurs), precise and measured approaches to decisions and work process (administrators), empathetic and team-focused (integrators), and individuals who are results and task oriented but not engaged with process (producers). Nuances abound and one should not be too wedded to these descriptors, but as you look at team composition, consider how these styles will impact decision making.

DISC
https://discpersonalitytesting.com/free-disc-test/

Kolb Learning Style Inventory
https://aim.stanford.edu/wp-content/uploads/2013/05/Kolb
-Learning-Style-Inventory.pdf

True Colors
http://www.truecolorsworkshops.com/test/true-colors-quick
-assessment-test/

Appendix B

HYPOTHETICAL EXERCISES: LEADING UP

These scenarios reflect real-life issues faced by individuals working at museums as shared with the author. Consider how you as an individual, or along with others in your organization, might resolve these dilemmas. As expected there is not one right answer.

1. Between the mid-level and top level of the museum there is a toxic personality who is paranoid and has a lot of power. We want to empower our department in the eyes of the top managers. How do we work through or around this individual?
2. How do you tell your boss that the task they assigned is not possible given the timing or resources without angering her? How do you deliver bad news to the boss?
3. Every time we get a new director we have a new strategic plan. How can we get clarification and buy-in within our department?

4. My boss has authority as a vice president, but he is a poor manager and doesn't communicate effectively. How do we deal with this person who always takes credit for our good ideas?

5. I have ideas to improve our programs in the museum. How do I get opportunities to take on new projects and move up the ladder?

Appendix C

TEAM DECISION-MAKING EXERCISE

The Metro Museum is located in an older part of the city on the edge of a neighborhood renewal program that will include a sports stadium, art galleries, and upscale restaurants. The museum building is a registered landmark (a former library) and has been undergoing renovations for the past year to add new classrooms, a changing gallery, and improved HVAC systems. The museum has completed about 50 percent of the needed renovations. Funding has come from state and federal grants as well as corporate donations. The museum is conducting a low-key campaign but has struggled within a competitive philanthropic environment. The annual operating budget is based on revenues from contributions and an annual giving campaign, memberships, and a small gift shop. The museum has a modest endowment of $10 million. In the past two years economic reversals have led to declining funding and the museum has cut back on programming and staffing. A budget of $1.5 million has shrunk to $1 million. The board has authorized a deficit budget. The museum is free to the public, but has cut back on its hours in order to save money. A staff of twenty full time and part time work in the museum caring for its 10,000 artifacts, managing a few annual exhibitions and educational programs. Attendance has dropped about 50 percent due to the renovations and the lack of changing exhibitions. Staff morale has been poor. Raises have been frozen and the director has talked about furloughing the staff one day a month. Some of the staff have talked about forming a union to protect their interests, while others (the more creative and energetic) are actively looking for new jobs. Communications among museum departments has been poor.

You are a member of the senior management team, which includes the director and department heads. The following issues appear on your agenda at your weekly meeting. The director has asked that the team review these issues, decide what action is needed, and which are priorities. What is urgent and what is important? Can anything be dealt with quickly? What needs further study? Who will be responsible for dealing with these issues? Are there policies in place to help with decisions?

Issues

1. The curator of the exhibition "Civil War Heroes in Metro" has sent the director, Martin Sureright, an email about the pistol problem. Two of the nineteenth-century pistols donated by General Ramrod, slated to be in the exhibition opening next week, are nowhere to be found. The registrar is on sick leave and General Ramrod is due at the museum in the afternoon to get a sneak preview of the exhibition.
2. A phone message was left on the director's voice mail noting that the mayor of Metro was calling a special city council meeting at the end of the week to discuss funding a major new educational program—a one-time matching grant to create school programs on the topic of minorities in sport. This will coincide with the opening of the new Corona Stadium in three months. "Interested parties should come to the meeting with ideas."
3. The *Metro Post* arts reporter sent an email to director Sureright asking for an interview about the museum's plan to deaccession a prized Monet landscape. The museum board has approved this

action based on its lack of relevance to the mission of Metro. Some staff have been concerned about how the proceeds will be used.

4. Mike Mantle, curator of sports and popular culture, just had a conversation with his boss, chief curator Sally Smart. He was very angry about two things: (1) the budget for special exhibitions was cut again this year and (2) staff morale problems at the museum. He feels that funding for renovations has taken precedence over the need to give the staff raises and do "serious work." He said "we need to get equity for all the staff or we will take to the streets in protest." Mike is known as a hot head, and an active member of @MuseumWorkersRevolt. The staff seems to listen to him.

5. Board chairman Bob Bagabucks is scheduled to meet with director Sureright the following day for lunch. Bob has been working with the development director, Ivana Geft, on some ideas about moving forward on the capital campaign for building renovations. He thinks that some local corporations would provide funding for a new 4-d interactive virtual reality theater. He told Sureright "Giving them a naming opportunity would be all that's needed."

The museum departments include Curatorial, Education, Administration, and Development. Assume the role of one of the department heads. Consider which of the five issues is the most pressing, how it should be resolved, and how you will work with your fellow management committee members and the director to resolve it. How do the other issues get resolved? Do this exercise in a team.

SELECTED
BIBLIOGRAPHY

Abram, Ruth J. "History Is as History Does: The Evolution of a Mission-Driven Museum." In *Looking Reality in the Eye*, edited by Robert Janes and Gerald Conaty, 19–42. Calgary: University of Calgary Press, 2005.

Ackerson, Anne W., and Joan H. Baldwin. *Leadership Matters*. Lanham, MD: AltaMira Press, 2014.

Adizes, Ichak. *Managing Corporate Life Cycles*. Paramus, NJ: Prentice Hall, 1999.

Anderson, Gail. *Museum Mission Statements: Building a Distinct Identity*. Washington, DC: American Association of Museums, 1998.

Baldwin, Joan, and Anne Ackerson. *Women in the Museum: Lessons from the Workplace*. New York: Routledge, 2017.

Bennett, Nathan, and Stephen A. Miles. "Second in Command, the Misunderstood Role of the Chief Operating Officer." *Harvard Business Review* 84, no. 5 (2006): 71–78.

Bennis, Warren. *Why Leaders Can't Lead*. Reading, MA: Addison-Wesley, 1989.

Bergeron, Anne, and Beth Tuttle. *Magnetic: The Art and Science of Engagement*. Washington, DC: American Association of Museums, 2013.

Bolman, Lee G., and Terrence E. Deal. *Reframing Organizations*. New York: John Wiley, 2008.

Bridges, William. *Managing Transitions*. Reading, MA: Addison-Wesley, 1991.

Brown, Tim. *Change by Design: How Design Thinking Transforms Organizations and Inspires Innovation*. New York: HarperCollins, 2009.

Bryan, Charles F. "Stages in the Life of a Museum Director." *Museum News* (January/February 2007): 54–59.

Case, John. *Open Book Management*. New York: HarperBusiness, 1995.

Collins, James C. *Good to Great*. New York: HarperBusiness, 2001.

———. *Good to Great and the Social Sectors: Why Business Thinking Is Not the Answer*. Jim Collins, 2005.

Collins, James C., and Jerry Porras. *Built to Last*. New York: HarperBusiness, 1997.

Dearstyne, Bruce. *Leading the Historical Enterprise*. Lanham, MD: Rowman & Littlefield, 2015.

Drucker, Peter. *Managing the Nonprofit Organization*. New York: HarperCollins, 1990.

Durel, John, and Will Phillips. *The Deputy's Handbook*. n.p.: Qm², 2002.

Edmondson, Amy. *Teaming: How Organizations Learn, Innovate, and Compete in the Knowledge Economy*. San Francisco: Jossey-Bass, 2012.

Falk, John, and Beverly Sheppard. *Thriving in the Knowledge Age*. Lanham, MD: AltaMira Press, 2006.

Ferrin, Richard. "The Time Between: A Report of Museum Interim Executive Leadership Patterns." Los Angeles: Arts Consulting Group, 2002.

Genoways, Hugh, Lynne M. Ireland, and Cinnamon Catlin-Legutko. *Museum Administration 2.0*. Lanham, MD: Rowman & Littlefield, 2017.

Gilmore, Thomas N. *Making a Leadership Change*. San Francisco: Jossey-Bass, 1989.

Goleman, Daniel. "Leadership That Gets Results." *Harvard Business Review* 78, no. 2 (2000): 78–90.

Goler, Robert. "Interim Directorships in Museums: Their Impact on Individuals and Significance to Institutions." *Museum Management and Curatorship* 19, no. 4 (2004): 385–402.

Grant, Adam. *Originals: How Non-Conformists Move the World*. New York: Viking, 2016.

Greenleaf, Robert K. *Servant Leadership*. New York: Paulist Press, 1977.

Gurian, Elaine Heumann. *Institutional Trauma*. Washington, DC: American Association of Museums, 1995.

Heath, Chip, and Dan Heath. *Switch: How to Change Things When Change in Hard*. New York: Broadway Books, 2010.

———. *Decisive: How to Make Better Choices in Work and Life*. New York: Crown Business, 2013.

HBR. *Guide to Managing Up and Across.* Boston: Harvard Business Review Press, 2013.

Heifetz, Ronald, and Donald Laurie. *The Practice of Adaptive Leadership.* Boston: Harvard Business Press, 2009.

Huy, Quy Nguyen. "In Praise of Middle Managers." *Harvard Business Review* 79, no. 8 (2001): 72–79.

Illinois Arts Alliance Foundation. *Succession: Arts Leadership for the 21st Century.* Report. 2002.

Janes, Robert. *Museums in a Troubled World.* New York: Routledge, 2009.

———. *Museums and the Paradox of Change.* New York: Routledge, 2013.

———. *Museums without Borders.* New York: Routledge, 2016.

Jung, Yuha. "Micro Examination of Museum Workplace Culture: How Institutional Changes Influence the Culture of a Real-World Art Museum." *Museum Management and Curatorship* 21, no. 2 (2016): 159–177.

Kaiser, Michael, and Bret E. Egan. *The Cycle: A Practical Approach to Managing Arts Organizations.* Waltham, MA: Brandeis University Press, 2013.

Katzenbach, Jon R., and Douglas K. Smith. *The Wisdom of Teams.* New York: HarperBusiness, 1993.

Kotter, John. *Leading Change.* Boston: Harvard Business School Press, 1996.

LaPiana, David. *The Nonprofit Strategy Revolution.* St. Paul, MN: Fieldstone, 2008.

Leiby, Maria Quinlan. "Choosing Middle Management." *History News* 58, no. 4 (2003): 12–14.

Liedtka, Jeanne, A. King, and K. Bennett. *Solving Problems with Design Thinking.* New York: Columbia University Press, 2013.

Lord, Gail. *Cities, Museums and Soft Power.* Washington, DC: American Alliance of Museums, 2015.

Lord, Gail, and Kate Markert. *The Manual of Strategic Planning for Cultural Organizations.* Lanham, MD: Rowman & Littlefield, 2017.

Marquardt, Michael. *Action Learning.* Palo Alto, CA: Davies Black, 2009.

Morris, Martha. "Vision, Values, Voice: The Leadership Challenge." In *Museum Studies,* edited by Stephen Williams and Catharine A. Hawks, 35–46. Society for the Preservation of Natural History Collections, 2006.

———. *Managing People and Projects in Museums: Strategies That Work.* Lanham, MD: Rowman & Littlefield, 2017.

Myerson, Debra. *Tempered Radicals: How Everyday Leaders Inspire Change at Work.* Cambridge: Harvard Business School Press, 2003.

Norris, Linda, and Rainey Tisdale. *Creativity in Museum Practice.* Walnut Creek, CA: Left Coast Press, 2014.

Peters, Tom, and Robert Waterman. *In Search of Excellence.* New York: Harper and Row, 1982.

Rorschach, Kimerly. *Know Before You Go.* New York: Center for Curatorial Leadership, 2017.

Senge, Peter. *The Fifth Discipline: The Art and Practice of the Learning Organization.* New York: Doubleday, 1990.

Shapiro, Michael. *Eleven Museum Directors: Conversations on Art and Leadership.* Atlanta: High Museum of Art, 2015.

Simon, Nina. *The Art of Relevance.* Santa Cruz, CA: Museum 2.0, 2016.

Stevens, Greg, and Wendy Luke. *A Life in Museums, Managing Your Museum Career.* Washington, DC: American Association of Museums, 2012.

Suchy, Sherene. *Leading with Passion: Change Management in the 21st Century Museum.* Lanham, MD: AltaMira Press, 2004.

Useem, Michael. *Leading Up.* New York: Crown Business, 2001.

Willyerd, Karie, and Barbara Mistick. *Stretch: How to Future-Proof Yourself for Tomorrow's Workplace.* Hoboken, NJ: John Wiley and Sons, 2016.

INDEX

ABOUT THE AUTHOR
AND THE CONTRIBUTORS

Martha Morris is associate professor emeritus of museum studies at the George Washington University in Washington, D.C. She has over 45 years of experience in the museum field as a manager and leader. Her career began in registration and collections management at the Corcoran Gallery of Art and later at the Smithsonian's Museum of American History where she eventually served as deputy director. Her work and her teaching have consistently focused on management and leadership practices, including strategic planning, project management, teambuilding, staff development, and facilities projects. As a member of the board of the Midatlantic Association of Museums she served as founding program chair of the annual Building Museums symposium. She has designed workshops, lectured and written on a number of topics including collections planning and management, exhibition development, leading change, museum facilities programs, museum mergers, and 21st century leadership skills. She is author of *Managing People and Projects in Museums* (2017) and co-author of *Planning Successful Museum Building Projects* (2009). She holds BA and MA degrees in Art History and a Master's in Business Administration.

Michelle Delaney is the senior program officer for History and Culture, Office of the Provost, Smithsonian Institution. Delaney is leading signature programs expansion in the Grand Challenges areas of Understanding the American Experience and Valuing World Cultures, and provides executive administrative and programmatic leadership for the nine Smithsonian American history and culture museums and research centers. Previously Delaney was director for the Smithsonian Consortia for the Humanities, and curator of photography at the National Museum of American History. Delaney has authored and edited several photography books, and curated more than 20 Smithsonian exhibitions and related web projects. She is a current board member for the Buffalo Bill Center of the West, and History PhD. candidate at the University of Strathclyde, Glasgow, Scotland.

Elizabeth Kirby is the grant development specialist in the Office of the Provost and Under Secretary for Museums and Research at the Smithsonian. She works with interdisciplinary research projects and assists with funding source research and proposal development. Prior to joining the Smithsonian, she was the director of the Office of Sponsored Programs at American University. She also worked in the university's development office in corporate and foundation relations and held a post in Continuing Education that involved teaming with faculty to develop customized training and education programs for private and public sector organizations. She is a member of the National Organization of Research Development Professionals and holds the Certified Research Administrator (CRA) credential. She has an MA in Linguistics from American University and a BA in Asian Studies from the University of Florida.

Jillian Jones holds a BA in Anthropology from the State University of New York at Geneseo and an MA in Museum Studies from the George Washington University. At GW, she focused her graduate studies in resource development and administration for non-profit institutions. She holds a certificate in Fundraising Management from the Lilly School of Philanthropy at Indiana University–Purdue University. She has been working in the field of philanthropy since 2006, first in higher education and then in arts and culture. She spent five years at the Virginia Museum of Fine Arts in Richmond, Virginia, as the manager of individual giving, leading the team responsible for identifying, soliciting, and stewarding large and small gifts to support exhibition and education programs from individual patrons. She has served as the director of advancement at the Albright-Knox Art Gallery in Buffalo, New York, since March 2015 where she leads a team of nine people responsible for raising an average $5 million annually while simultaneously conducting a $155 million capital campaign—the largest the museum has ever undertaken. She also sits on the museum's executive leadership team.

Erin Carlson Mast is CEO and executive director of President Lincoln's Cottage in Washington, DC. She was a member of the original team leading to the Cottage's grand opening in 2008. Since 2010, Mast has led the organization through growth, groundbreaking programming, and significant recognition, including a Presidential Medal and being named one of Washington, DC's, 50 Best Places to work and the Best Museum off the Mall. In 2016, she led the organization through its transition to an independent 501(c)(3). Mast has written for such publications as *History News* and *The Public Historian* and was a contributing author to *Museums of Ideas: Commitment and Conflict* (MuseumsEtc, 2011). She holds an MA in Museum Studies from The George Washington University and a BA in History from the Ohio University Honors Tutorial College.

April Salomon is executive director of the Musical Instrument Museum in Phoenix, Arizona. Joining the organization in 2007, Ms. Salomon played an integral role in the design, staffing, collection acquisition, and launch of the $250 million museum before taking the helm in May 2014. Having worked extensively in both public and private sectors, Ms. Salomon held positions at the Smithsonian Institution, Intel Corporation, Hewlett-Packard, Heard Museum, Institute for Learning Innovation, and Newseum. She also received her BA in Art History from the University of California at Davis, MA in Museum Studies from George Washington University, an MBA with a non-profit focus from the University of St. Thomas, Minneapolis, and received certification from Harvard Business School for completing *Strategic Perspectives in Non-Profit Management*.

Lauren Shenfeld is manager of public programs at The Children's Museum of Atlanta. Prior to this role, Lauren served as the director of special projects at EdVenture Children's Museum in Columbia, South Carolina. Lauren initially joined EdVenture in May 2015 as director of museum experiences, overseeing visitor services and public programming. Prior to this, Lauren served as a Presidential Administrative Fellow at the George Washington University Museum and The Textile Museum where she aided in the historic move and reopening of The Textile Museum at GW and the development of the new GW Museum. Lauren received her MA in Museum Studies in 2015. She currently co-chairs the leadership committee for Emerging Museum Professionals of the Southeastern Museums Conference.

Sandra Smith is the vice president of engagement and enterprise at the Senator John Heinz History Center in Pittsburgh, Pa. Prior to this position she served as founding director of Villa Finale in San Antonio, Texas, and director of museum collections for the National Trust for Historic Preservation in Washington, DC. Smith also serves on the AASLH editorial board. She holds degrees in Classical Studies and Museum Studies.